ONE *Million People* OUT OF DEBT

MISSION ONE MILLION

™

CREATING WEALTH
ONE *Family at a Time*

Merle Gilley and Steve Burton

HUGO HOUSE PUBLISHERS, LTD.

ISBN: 978-1-948261-06-7

Trademark Information

The "S&P 500" and the "Dow Jones Industrial Average" are products of S&P Dow Jones Indices LLC ("SPDJI"). Standard & Poor's®, S&P® and S&P 500® are registered trademarks of Standard & Poor's Financial Services LLC ("S&P"); DJIA®, The Dow®, Dow Jones® and Dow Jones Industrial Average are trademarks of Dow Jones Trademark Holdings LLC ("Dow Jones"); and these trademarks have been licensed for use by SPDJI.

This book is not sponsored, endorsed, sold or promoted by SPDJI, Dow Jones, S&P, their respective affiliates, and none of such parties make any representation regarding the advisability of investing in such product(s) nor do they have any liability for any errors, omissions, or interruptions of the S&P 500 or the Dow Jones Industrial Average.

Cover Design: Monica Gilley

Interior Layout: Ronda Taylor, Heartwork Publishing

Hugo House Publishers, Ltd.

H+H

Austin, TX • Denver, CO
www.hugohousepublishers.com

Limits of Liability

The author and publisher shall not be liable for misuse of this material. This book is strictly for informational and educational purposes.

Disclaimer

While great efforts have been taken to provide accurate and current information regarding the covered material, neither the authors, TriQuest USA, Equity 1 Inc Financial Solutions, or any affiliates are responsible for any errors or omissions, or for the results or lack of results obtained from the use of this information.

Every effort has been made to accurately represent these products and their potential. However, there is no guarantee that you will earn any money using the techniques and ideas in these materials. Examples in these materials are not to be interpreted as a promise or guarantee of earnings. Earning potential is entirely dependent on the person using our product, ideas, and techniques. We do not purport this as a "get rich scheme."

Your level of success in attaining the results claimed in our materials depends on the time you devote to the program, ideas and techniques mentioned, your finances, knowledge, and various skills. Since these factors differ according to individuals, we cannot guarantee your success or income level, nor are we responsible for any of your actions.

Materials in our products may contain information that includes or is based upon forward-looking statements. Any and all forward-looking statements here or on any of our material are intended to express our opinion of earnings potential. Many factors will be important in determining your actual results and no guarantees are made that you will achieve results similar to ours or anybody else's; in fact, no guarantees are made that you will achieve any results from our ideas and techniques in our material.

The ideas, suggestions, general principles and conclusions presented here are subject to local, state and federal laws and regulations and revisions of same and are intended for informational purposes only. All information in *Mission ONE Million* is provided "as is," with no guarantee of completeness, accuracy, or timeliness regarding the results obtained from the use of this information.

The permanent life insurance products discussed in this book are not stock market investments. They do not directly participate in any stock or equity investments and do not receive dividend or capital gains participation. They are insurance policies that have accumulation accounts linked to a financial index. Their performance varies based on the product used, method of funding, size of policy, and performance of an index; past index performance is no indication of future crediting rates. All life insurance policies have sales charges, maintenance fees and the cost of insurance. Interest crediting fluctuations can lead to the need for additional premium in a life insurance policy. All permanent life insurance products should be reviewed with a competent and licensed financial services professional before they are purchased.

YOU EXPRESSLY ACKNOWLEDGE AND AGREE THAT USE OF AND RELIANCE ON THE INFORMATION IS AT YOUR SOLE RISK AND THAT THE ENTIRE RISK AS TO SATISFACTION, RESULTS, PERFORMANCE, ACCURACY AND EFFORT IS WITH YOU. TO THE MAXIMUM EXTENT PERMITTED BY APPLICABLE LAW. ALL INFORMATION IS PROVIDED "AS IS," WITH ALL FAULTS AND WITHOUT WARRANTY OF ANY KIND, AND THE AUTHORS OR THEIR AFFILIATES HEREBY DISCLAIM ALL WARRANTIES AND CONDITIONS WITH RESPECT TO THE PRODUCTS, EITHER EXPRESS, IMPLIED, OR STATUTORY, INCLUDING, BUT NOT LIMITED TO, THE IMPLIED WARRANTIES AND/OR CONDITIONS OF MERCHANTABILITY, SATISFACTORY QUALITY, FITNESS FOR A PARTICULAR PURPOSE, ACCURACY, QUIET ENJOYMENT, AND NON-INFRINGEMENT OF THIRD PARTY RIGHTS.

TO THE EXTENT NOT PROHIBITED BY LAW, IN NO EVENT SHALL THE AUTHOR, TriQuest USA, Equity 1 Inc. Financial Solutions OR THEIR AFFILIATES BE LIABLE FOR ANY DIRECT, INCIDENTAL, SPECIAL, INDIRECT OR CONSEQUENTIAL DAMAGES, LOSS OF PROFITS, LOSS OF DATA, BUSINESS INTERRUPTION OR ANY OTHER DAMAGES OR LOSSES, ARISING OUT OF OR RELATED TO YOUR USE OF THE PRODUCTS, HOWEVER CAUSED, REGARDLESS OF THE THEORY OF LIABILITY (CONTRACT, TORT OR OTHERWISE) AND EVEN IF THE AUTHOR OR PUBLISHER HAS BEEN ADVISED OF THE POSSIBILITY OF SUCH DAMAGES.

Dedication

To all those seeking the wisdom to free themselves from the burden of debt and striving to achieve financial independence.

Contents

BONUS CHAPTERS:

Introduction

The Mission Defined

WE ARE SWIMMING IN DEBT, BUT FEW OF US WANT TO admit it.

We are in debt because we spent too much on whatever it was that we just had to *have* at that moment. But the fact is, we lose a certain amount of freedom when we're under the burden of debt—a bunch of freedom. We're actually put into a state of servitude—to the lender, to the interest, or to the time period between loan payments.

Debt is a vicious cycle that shackles us. We begin our lives hoping for the very best. We embark on our career, but at some point, that career becomes a necessity. We *have* to keep that job to maintain the lifestyle we've created. But no matter how much we earn, it somehow is never enough. Why?

As we earn more money, we buy bigger houses, nicer cars, and resort vacations. We send our kids to college, pay for their weddings, and we watch whatever savings we managed to accumulate disappear as our debts mount higher and higher. But it's embarrassing to look all that debt square in the eye, so we continue to hope for the best while the burden grows heavier and heavier.

Debt doesn't magically disappear if we're unable to generate more income. The chains of debt most certainly don't fall away when we stop working. Debt continues to accumulate interest, and the bills demand to be paid no matter what.

At some point, we reflect on our choices and sadly realize, "There's no money." Instead there's a looming avalanche of debt that is threatening to bury us alive.

How We Manage Our Money

The way most of us have been taught to manage our money does NOT work. If it did, why would two out of three Americans think getting out of debt in their lifetime will never happen to them?

Here's the real truth. We're doing it wrong! That's because we haven't been taught or we're too lazy to learn how to manage money…the right way.

Consider Tom and Debbie. He's a police officer; she's an administrative aide. They are part of the 75 percent of Americans who make $75,000 or less.

Like most Americans, they used credit to have nice things. But they had over $30,000 of debt (and that wasn't including their mortgage), living paycheck to paycheck, and constantly stressed about money.

> The way most of us have been taught to manage our money does NOT work. If it did, why would two out of three Americans think getting out of debt in their lifetime will never happen to them?

They tried other debt-management programs, even attempted the "snowball effect" (what Steve calls the "slowball effect") where you take the lowest balance you have and apply extra principal payments until it's paid off. Then you keep marching up your list of debts until all of them are paid.

It didn't work for them. Just as it doesn't work for others, by the way. Sometimes, it takes too long, and the person can't stay that disciplined. We've also had people say that it helped get them out of debt, but it didn't keep them debt free for long.

Whatever the case for Tom and Debbie, the credit-card interest was killing them. But they were serious about getting out of debt, staying out of debt, and doing something responsible

> They had more money going out than coming in every month, and they were increasing the amount of their debt monthly.

with their money. They heard about our Mission ONE Million program and wanted to try it.

When we ran their numbers in our program, we discovered they had a negative cash flow. They had more money going out than coming in every month, and they were increasing the amount of their debt monthly. It's a common problem, but would that disqualify them from participating in the Mission ONE Million program?

It's Not Magic. It's Math

The Mission ONE Million system isn't magic. It's math. Debt elimination can ONLY happen if you have a positive cash flow—meaning you have money left over after you pay your bills. Too many Americans, when they have positive cash flow, end up spending it. Even if they save the extra cash, they don't know what to do with it.

> Too many Americans, when they have positive cash flow, end up spending it. Even if they save the extra cash, they don't know what to do with it.

But what would happen if they took the difference between what they make and what they spend on bills and use that discretionary cash, the same thing as positive cash flow, to eliminate debt first?

We gave Tom and Debbie a homework assignment: either get part-time jobs or go home, sharpen their pencil, and find some discretionary income. We never expected to see them again.

A couple months later they called our office. They had done their homework and asked us to rerun the numbers. They had done it! They took responsibility for their money, reorganized their spending, and created the positive cash flow necessary to go into the debt-elimination portion of the Mission ONE Million program.

The transformation was remarkable. In just over a year, they had canceled out tens of thousands of dollars in credit-card debt and were able to create a $20,000 plus emergency fund. But here's the most exciting part. Because they had eliminated their debt, they could now do something people too often think is reserved for the wealthy. They still had the same jobs, but credit card payments and other bad debt weren't eating up their monthly income. So they went from having nothing saved to putting over $1,000 a month in a special accumulation account that continually earns compounding interest.

In other words, they were creating wealth.

Tom and Debbie are now well on their way to having $40,000 to $50,000 a year of income in retirement. Because they took the time to learn how to manage their cash flow, they now live without the overwhelming stress of debt. More importantly, they learned how to manage the surplus effectively. And their special accumulation account will not only provide enough interest for them to live on when they retire or are not able to work, they can also access their money tax free and without market risk whenever they want, with no restrictions.

Here's the best part. As they continue to eliminate debt, they can put more money into their special accumulation account. This will give them an even greater cash reserve earning interest.

Think about how that would feel—not being burdened with debt, not having to worry about money, not wondering how you're going to pay for college, or a hospital visit, or how you're going to live comfortably without taking on a part-time job. It's freeing.

It's something most Americans dream about or envy, spending *billions* of dollars on the lottery hoping their numbers will hit. But deep down, they have convinced themselves that a debt-free life is something they will never experience. Creating wealth is way beyond their wildest dreams. So they accept the burden and "habit" of debt.

Mission ONE Million

We have collectively watched too many lives crash because people were not financially prepared for retirement.

We have also helped thousands of people get out of debt. They were able to create positive cash flow. That plus discipline and perseverance helped them create one million dollars (or more!) in a special interest-bearing accumulation account. It's earning uninterrupted compounding interest that is not subject to market risk, or future taxation.

What do these people do with this million dollars? Most leave it in the special accumulation account but can chose to fund all those things they want or need. Most of all, they are excited about living worry-free! The interest they're now earning pays them just as much as their salary did when they were working—and sometimes more.

That's financial independence. It's the byproduct of creating positive cash flow, *and* it's also the mission!

The push for people to take that kind of control in their financial lives prompted Mission ONE Million—one million people out of debt and creating wealth with one million dollars in a special accumulation account.

Our goal is to change the way Middle America handles their money. We know it's possible. We have already helped thousands!

Make It Your Own

We have found over the years that it doesn't matter if you're making $60,000 a year or $300,000 a year. If you're not paying attention, your spending "habits" will meet your income. So, while Mission ONE Million is targeted toward those who need it most—the 75 percent of people who make $75,000 or less—it's a mission anyone can accomplish!

- If you're living paycheck to paycheck and constantly stress about money...
- If your bills are late so you're working late but missing your son and his soccer game, again...

- If you miss a monthly payment and the credit card company is calling you three times a day...
- If you had zero interest credit cards, but the grace period is up so you're charged an astronomical amount of interest...
- If you've overextended yourself on your mortgage and car payment, so you can't pay your bills—let alone your daughter's wedding...
- If a night out with friends causes stress because you don't have the freedom to spend an extra $50...
- If you want more, less, different, or better...we encourage you to keep reading.

When you use positive cash flow to create wealth, that freedom becomes opportunity—to create more wealth and thereby do more good for you and your family, your neighborhood, your church, even the world.

If you get your cash flow under control, that creates freedom. An extra five-hundred to a thousand dollars a month might be a tremendous relief! But there's more where that came from.

When you use positive cash flow to create wealth, that freedom becomes opportunity—to create more wealth and thereby do more good for you and your family, your neighborhood, your church, even the world. That's what America was built on—freedom. Isn't it time you found yours?

By the way, this can all happen without a lot of sacrifice. You have to be smart and responsible with your money. You have to follow the Mission ONE Million program to get the results Tom and Debbie have enjoyed. But it can be done.

You can be something more than a servant to your debt. You can do those things you want. You can have an abundant life.

To live financially independent is the mission!

ONE

The Debt Threat: Why You Need to Protect Your Cash Flow

Do YOU REALIZE THAT YOUR LARGEST ASSET IS YOUR cash flow? People will proudly list their assets as houses, 401(k)'s, managed fund accounts (if they have them), but they never look at cash flow. Cash flow, over the course of a working lifetime, dwarfs everything—often even when all the assets are combined.

Say you earn an average of $40,000 a year over the course of your working years. You started out making less than that, hopefully got raises over the years, and retired making more. But say the average is $40K. Multiplied by forty years—the amount of time most people work, twenty-five through sixty-five—that's $1.6 million. That's a lot of money considering $40,000 a year

> Cash flow, over the course of a working lifetime, dwarfs everything ...

1

isn't a lot of money when it comes to managing the average American household.

Now imagine there's a pipe that runs throughout your home. It comes in the front door and moves through your house, splitting off into the various rooms: the kitchen, living room, bedroom, home office, garage, and even the bathrooms.

This pipeline represents your cash flow, and your paycheck keeps the pipeline flowing. At each room, the money in the pipe flows out through various spigots. There's food in the kitchen, stereos and TV/internet in the living room, clothes and bedding in the bedrooms, toiletries in the bathroom, cars, including the insurance, and toys in the garage. (And toys aren't just for kids. Your jet skis, snowboards, etc. count.) You get the idea.

Out of the spigots in each room flows money to pay for all those "things" in your home. Some are necessary, some aren't. Money flows, nonetheless.

Your mortgage has a special pipe directly to your mortgage company. If you have debt, there's another pipeline diverted to the bank or to the credit card companies. The more you buy on credit, the bigger the pipe as it diverts the money you commit to payments. But there's only so much money in that pipeline. Remember, it's fed by your paycheck. So the more your money flows to the bank to pay debt, the less money you have to buy necessities, like food, and things you want or need such as shoes and clothes.

Now here's the question. How much money is left flowing out the end of the pipe when you're done paying for everything?

For too many households, there's absolutely nothing left over, not even a trickle! Millions of dollars of cash flow, siphoned off by bad debt.

> For too many households, there's absolutely nothing left over, not even a trickle! Millions of dollars of cash flow, siphoned off by bad debt.

The (little) Money ...Trap!

No one likes debt. But how many times have you looked at something you wanted—even something seemingly insignificant like a new pair of shoes—realized you didn't have enough money to buy it, and whipped out your credit card?

We are all guilty of it.

We use credit cards for all sorts of "big" things: vacations, smart HD TVs, or new furniture. But is it wise to use a credit card to make up the difference between what we make and what we want?

> Is it wise to use a credit card to make up the difference between what we make and what we want?

3

Oftentimes we'll stop at the local convenience store to grab a newspaper. There will be several people at the counter buying breakfast and loading up on things for the day. Most of the time, they pay with a credit card. They're charging $10, $20, even $30 every day, not realizing how much those charges are really costing them.

> They're charging $10, $20, even $30 every day, not realizing how much those charges are really costing them.

We hear it all the time, "If you just pay the minimum, you're never going to get ahead." But we do it anyway. Let's look at how true that statement is. Those $30 convenience stops…that $50 for games…the $100 for shoes…. Your credit cards charge you interest, ranging from 0 to over 30 percent! Let's say you're at the higher end, 24.9 percent APR, because your credit score is just fair (the higher scores get the lower 12 percent APR).

The "Annual Percentage Rate" (APR) is the amount of interest charged on the balance of the card over one year. However, if the balance is paid in full each month, they do not charge interest.

Suppose you run the balance up to $7,000 and only pay the minimum monthly payment of $149. If you made no more charges, it would take fifteen years to pay your credit card off…and close to $20,000 in interest!

Suppose you run the balance up to $7,000 and only pay the minimum monthly payment of $149. If you made no more charges, it would take fifteen years to pay your credit card off…and close to $20,000 in interest!

So whatever you bought for $7,000 actually costs you $27,000.

Remember the cash flow pipe running through your house? That's $20,000 diverted to a credit card company, making your cash flow slow to a trickle.

And a $7,000 credit card balance is low for most people!

Take the time to add up to how much you owe and enter all the minimum payments/interest rates on a credit card calculator website. You'll be startled at how much money you're *losing* to credit card interest. It's a shameful number. But do you really SEE how much cash flow you're losing over the course of that credit card expense?

If you made $5,000 a month and you spent $5,000 a month, how much do you have left? Nothing.

If you made $5,000 a month and spent $5,300, where's the extra $300 coming from? Credit cards usually.

How much will a $50 or a $300 or even a $2,000 charge cost you over the long haul? A lot. Most likely, more than you have. That's why debt hurts so much. It's a trap. It kills your cashflow, and that kills opportunity.

> That's why debt hurts so much. It's a trap.
> It kills your cashflow, and that kills opportunity.

The Cost of Lost Opportunity

There's a car dealership on the main road to our offices. They have figured out the game. They routinely put a price on a car, say $349 per month. But if no one buys the car, they put a new sign on it that advertises $87 per week. The two-digit figure on a shiny car appears to be a much more reasonable expense, so the likelihood of them selling it skyrockets.

Marketers know that if they break down a larger figure into smaller payments, consumers are more likely to justify their desire to acquire. They may not need it—but they sure do want it. What's an extra $80 a week anyway?

> Marketers know that if they break down a larger figure into smaller payments, consumers are more likely to justify their desire to acquire.

Thus, even more money is diverted from the cash flow pipeline.

In the introduction, we talked about how you can use money you're not spending (buying stuff you don't need or paying interest) to create wealth. See how this works in the pipeline? The less your money is diverted, the more your money flows to the end of the cash-flow pipe, increasing your opportunity to create wealth.

Every dollar you earn in your lifetime affords you basically two choices: Spend it on needs and wants. Or save it.

Let's go back to the convenience store. It's estimated that the average person will spend $3,000 a year on coffee and going out to breakfast and/or lunch. There are those who certainly spend more and some who spend less. Let's go with the average and say the young person has thirty years to go before they retire.

> ## It's estimated that the average person will spend $3,000 a year on coffee and going out to breakfast and/or lunch.

If that $3,000 was put into some sort of accumulation account instead, earning a conservative 7 percent interest, they would have over a quarter of a million dollars in savings at the end of their working years.

That…is opportunity.

But because they are spending it instead of saving it, opportunity is lost. They have nothing left but paper cups and dirty dishes. That's the cost of lost opportunity.

The idea behind Mission ONE Million is to create AND take advantage of opportunity, *and* avoid the cost of not knowing how to spend and save your money wisely.

We cannot stress this enough. Your cash flow is FAR more important than daily visits to the coffee shop. Every dollar you have today can be equivalent to $5 or $10 in the future. That $5 cup of joe that you buy at the fancy coffee shop today actually costs you upwards of $25 to $35! That's the amount of money you'd make over time if you invested the $5 instead of drinking it.

It's enough to make you think twice, when you consider the future dollar value of today's unnecessary expenses!

The Instant Gratification Trap

Around 70 percent of Americans are living paycheck to paycheck. It's *not* because they don't make enough money. It's because they don't have enough control over their cash flow.

People want the newest cell phone or the latest trend. They have to have all the things they desire, right now.

Why?

We all know it—instant gratification. It's the desire to have something *now* because it makes us feel good. It kind of feels like winning, and we like it! We experience a "winning sensation" when we spend, so we spend what we don't have—again and again.

> Around 70 percent of Americans are living paycheck to paycheck. It's not because they don't make enough money. It's because they don't have enough control over their cash flow.

In a way, it's like stealing. When we buy something on credit, we're stealing from our future cash flow, just so we can have, and feel, something *right now*. But that's not winning. That's losing—big time. And eventually, you do get caught. You have enormous credit card debt and not enough cash flow to handle it.

> When we buy something on credit, we're stealing from our future cash flow, just so we can have, and feel, something right now.

When two-income families became the norm, the phenomena of "keeping up with the Joneses" multiplied. Instead of saving any extra paycheck, families spent more...and more. Think of the pipeline: bigger houses, nicer cars, and more toys!

"Get rid of debt" websites might try to convince you that, "Debt is not how our grandparents did it. They saved, and only bought what they could afford." That's true to a certain extent, but the real reason why they didn't have a credit problem was they didn't use credit. If they did, it was rarely and they worked to pay if off as quickly as possible because debt was embarrassing and detrimental.

In times past, there was something called company "script." Miners were paid in script which could only be used in the company store—and the company store was smart. They extended script loans to the miners, knowing they couldn't pay it all back, ensuring the miners' "faithful" service to the company.

Tennessee Ernie Ford, a country-western singer in the 1940s and 50s, sang a hit song called, "Sixteen Tons." The miner works hard to load "sixteen tons" of coal every day for the company, but the refrain bemoans the heaviest burden of all…*debt*!

> You load sixteen tons, what do you get?
> Another day older and deeper in debt.
> Saint Peter, don't you call me, 'cause I can't go;
> I owe my soul to the company store.[1]

Debt is debt. It has always put the borrower in bondage to the lender, and it always will.

Federal law requires nutrition labels on packages so consumers are aware of the positive and/or negative impact on their health. It's supposed to help us make healthy choices. What if there were such a label on everything you bought that predicted how much money you would make by investing instead of spending it? That would never happen, of course, but it makes a point. You must consider the "financial health" of your spending.

> ## You must consider the "financial health" of your spending.

---

1   ©Unichappell. 1947. All rights reserved.

Good Debt versus Bad Debt

We need to learn how to respect our money. We also need to learn how to be disciplined enough *not* to spend money we don't have. It's the old-fashioned principle of "living within our means." It sounds restrictive, but you're the one in control.

You figure out how much money is coming into the cash-flow pipeline. You figure out what needs to flow to the various spigots to maintain the basic necessities. If this sounds like budgeting, you're right.

But there's one more thing to consider about debt. It's something we'll cover in much greater detail later in the book. For now, let's just say there's good debt and there's bad debt.

We've been talking about the bad debt, the kind of debt that siphons off too much of your cash flow, leaving you with nothing.

> But there is also a good debt.
> It's the kind of debt that can work for you.
> This debt even allows deductions on your income tax!

But there is also a good debt. It's the kind of debt that can work for you. This debt even allows deductions on your income tax! If you can deduct the interest from debt, then it has advantages—especially if you have the rest of your money earning interest in a tax-free and risk-free environment.

There's also another kind of debt that can actually help you build wealth. Both of these are good debt, and that's all we're going to say about it for now.

The Wealth Builder Account

Bad debt clogs up cash flow in the pipeline. That's why debt is so detrimental. You *must* pay the usual bills. You must also pay the bad debt to the credit card companies, whether you can "afford" the payment or not.

The old adage, "You must admit you have a problem before you can fix it," means to draw your attention to managing your debt. This chapter's mission is to help you *really see* how much cash flow you're losing because of debt. Once you realize what bad debt does to your cash flow, the next step is to do something about it—just like Tom and Debbie did—through the Mission ONE Million debt-elimination program.

They also began building wealth by flowing more and more cash into their special accumulation account. Let's look at that for a moment.

Let's say you figured out a way to have positive cash flow, meaning you actually have money flowing out the other end of the pipeline. Please do not make the mistake of spending that money on things you want (more shoes, toys, vacations) because you have it. That would be like pumping the extra cash flow right onto the ground—utterly wasted.

Like Tom and Debbie, you want that surplus to flow into savings, so you can create wealth. But in a bank? If that extra money flowed into a CD, it would earn hardly any interest, and even that interest would be taxed each year. So this may not be the wisest use of that extra cash flow.

Some may flow the money back into their mortgage. That may or may not be a wise choice. Some people put the extra into their IRA or 401(k) or other "qualified plans," which means you're just postponing the taxes until you take it out. If your employer is matching those funds, go for it. But here's the problem with a lot of qualified plans: they're tied to the stock market which puts your money at risk. This can (and has) deteriorated future cash flow.

There are many ways to save extra cash flow, but imagine, for instance, that you build a vault at the end of your pipeline. Say this vault allows you to earn a profitable rate of return, like 7 percent. Plus, it protects you from the risk of losing your money to market crashes or other adverse financial events like taxes.

This vault is our Wealth Builder account, the special accumulation account to which we've been referring. Chapter 6 explains it in detail, but here's an example of how it works:

Let's look at the $40,000-a-year scenario we opened with. You commit to putting 20 percent of your yearly earnings in your Wealth Builder account between your twenty-fifth and sixty-fifth birthday. If this account were earning 7 percent interest every year, and it was protected from loss, you would have $1.7 million in your Wealth Builder account at retirement (sixty-five). That's *more* money than you have made in your working years. And you can confidently live on the interest that $1.7 million is earning.

If you're thinking, "But I didn't start when I was twenty-five. I'm fifty-three. What can *I* do?" Well, let's say you make $60,000 a year. That's $5,000 a month. You commit to live on $3,000 a month so you can save $2,000, and you decide you're going to work until you're seventy-five because you started a little late in the game. On your retirement birthday, you will have $1 million in your Wealth Builder account. If that $1 million earns 6 percent a year, that could be enough to live on for the remainder of your life.

The Wealth Builder account represents a personal commitment to better financial health. For yourself, your family, and your future. That *is* the foundation of Mission ONE Million.

The Wealth Builder account represents a personal commitment to better financial health. For yourself, your family, and your future.

TWO

Take Back Control of Your Cash Flow

Have you ever felt like your debt has a personality? At first you feel as though you can control it.

But you've "entertained" debt so much, the debt now controls you. Its power over your life can have very tangible, even devastating, effects.

We know a small business owner who, at first, was very good at handling her cash flow. She was saving the money coming out the end of the cash-flow pipe, but then something happened. Her cash flow began to dwindle so she relied on the convenience of credit cards. As she diverted more of her cash flow toward debt, her debt took control of her life.

Millions of Americans just like her end up losing control because we are *encouraged to spend*. At every turn, we're

> Millions of Americans just like her end up losing control because we are encouraged to spend.

drawn to ads, ideas, or products that appeal to at least one (sometimes all) of our senses. And marketers know if they can get you to use a credit card, you will pay about 40 percent more than if you paid cash.

We feel bound and gagged by debt's interest and payments, and we want out! But how many of us never make a move to change our spending habits?

It's very much like a diet. You know you need to lose weight, but are you willing to change your eating habits to make that happen?

Eliminating debt begins with the discipline to create some positive cash flow. Get a little tough on yourself, and you'll feel debt beginning to lose its grip.

STEP ONE: Put Your Spending on a Diet

Just as there are a lot of ways to overeat, there are a lot of ways we overspend.

The very first thing you must figure out is where's the money going? What's your income minus your expenses? This includes your bills, food, gas, entertainment, even extra spending money.

This will help you *see* where your money is flowing—especially how much is going to "extra" spending and to debt. You might even notice that you can cut some over-spending on things like cable or phone.

Your primary focus is to cut down on "extra" spending. One of the easiest targets is food. How much are you spending on food and beverages outside the home?

- Instead of paying $2 to $6 for a cup of fancy coffee, brew your own at home. A cup of home-brewed coffee from a container of grounds costs around sixteen cents. For those of you who like the whole-bean fresh-ground stuff, it's eighteen cents. Add a couple of cents more for sugar and crème. Only go to the coffee shop as a treat.
- Pack your lunch for work. Instead of paying $10 to $15 for a salad, bring one from home. It'll cost a couple of bucks for the ingredients.
- There is a reason we used a convenience store in the Money Trap scenario. They're expensive! Never buy regular groceries at a convenience store. Do a cost comparison if you don't believe us.

There is a reason we used a convenience store in the Money Trap scenario. They're expensive! Never buy regular groceries at a convenience store.

- Make dinner or eat leftovers instead of ordering in or going out. Large meals, made in advance, are the best if both worlds: home-cooked, convenient, and you have lunch and dinner for days. This could save you $3,000 or more a year! That's a chunk of cash that can now flow into your Wealth Builder account.

- Instead of buying water or soda from a vending machine, buy it in bulk. Buy in bulk whenever you can. The big box membership stores have killer deals, and you can free up cash flow by taking advantage. The up-front cost is more, but the savings over time can be substantial.

- Alcohol can be a huge drain on the pocketbook. If you're going to drink, do so wisely. Don't run up huge tabs at the bar.

These changes alone will jump-start (or enhance) your cashflow, but there are lots more little ways to save big money.

Put yourself on a budget, and make sure you put some splurge money in there. It's okay to have an ice-cream once in a while. It's even okay to see a movie, go out for dinner, or enjoy a spa date with friends. But do it when you have the cash, and do it in moderation.

- Plan for the necessities. Your kids are going to need new clothes (or coats or fees for sports, etc.). So are you. Instead of waiting for the inevitable and charging those on a card because you can't afford to pay cash, open a "necessities" account and fund it monthly.

This is when banks are important. You don't want to put your "necessity" cash in the Wealth Builder account. That's the money you're saving for later. In the meantime, this small account can cover those things you may not need right now, but you know you're going to have to buy. A few hundred dollars in the account is all you need. The money is there when you need it—and make sure to stay disciplined and replenish it when the balance goes down.

- You should also be building an emergency fund so you don't have to use a credit card for life's inevitable disasters. You get a nail in your tire and have to repair or replace it. Your emergency fund can cover that. You get sick and can't work for a week—or a month. Your emergency fund is there to support you. And once again, you need to replenish it! It allows you to save now and spend less later.

- Most importantly, do not charge anything more on your credit cards. The idea here is to eliminate debt. Not create more.

> **Most importantly, do not charge anything more on your credit cards. The idea here is to eliminate debt. Not create more.**

We did a quick Web search for additional "ways to save money," and there were some great ideas. We encourage you to do your own searching. We don't have to "Keep up with the Kardashians," or fear we're going to miss out on something because we don't have the money.

"If you don't respect the small sums, you won't respect the large sums." The average person who goes on to create a million dollars or more of wealth is not some Wall-Street tycoon. They haven't won the lottery or opened some super successful business. This average person is just committed to making better financial decisions all the time.

> If you don't respect the small sums, you won't respect the large sums.

Spending habits can make us or break us, and what we're talking about here is life-style spending. We don't want to cramp your lifestyle. Rather, we're showing you that when you can put money back into the cash flow pipe, you keep money flowing instead of diverting it into extravagant spending sprees or paying minimum payments on overwhelming debt.

All this is designed to free up cash flow. Remember, Tom and Debbie couldn't start the debt-elimination program until they had positive cash flow. Their mission to get out of debt was accomplished through discipline. They put their spending on a diet and you saw the results. They now have their emergency fund, they're paying off thousands in credit-card debt, and they're adding to their Wealth Builder account.

Remember, he's a police officer and she's an administrative assistant. They are not wealthy people. If they can do it, you can too.

Remember, he's a police officer and she's an administrative assistant. They are not wealthy people. If they can do it, you can too.

STEP TWO: Use a Cash-Flow Management Software

There are a number of spreadsheet programs or phone apps that track your expenses. They can help, but we have found that people need something more.

The cash-flow management software we use helps direct your money more effectively. It keeps a close eye on where it goes and when it's spent, so you're keeping your payments on track, paying down debt, and ultimately creating more cash flow.

The cash-flow management software we use helps direct your money more effectively.

If you didn't have $500, $1,000, or even more in payments every month going to credit cards, your life would improve. This software speeds up the process, and the end result is more cash. Ideally, instead of letting your positive cash flow hit the ground, essentially wasting it, you direct it into your Wealth Builder account where it earns compounding interest and creates wealth.

The program requires only three things: a line of credit, a checking account (preferably at the same institution), and our software program. These three work in tandem with the discretionary income to pay off higher-interest debt. It's called financial leverage.

Using a line of credit might seem counter-intuitive, but it's not. To us, it's the twenty-first century "GPS" to achieving financial health. It's fast, effective, and it doesn't require a ton of sacrifice.

There are two basic ways you can get this low-interest line of credit. If you have equity in your home, you may qualify for a HELOC (home equity line of credit). Or you can open a personal line of credit. These are not "personal" loans which are paid to you in a lump sum. A line of credit comes into play only when you need it—or in this case, when the software tells you to use it.

> ## The software keeps you on track: How much to withdraw, when, and what debt to pay.

The software keeps you on track: How much to withdraw, when, and what debt to pay.

Step One was to determine your discretionary income. You either found money you didn't realize you had, or you reduced your spending enough to create additional cash flow. The program employs this "lazy money" to help drive down debt. "Lazy" money is anything that's left over after your bills and other expenses are paid.

You may be wasting this money or putting it in the bank to earn what we call "point nothing"—around one percent interest or less.) One of our clients described how our program turned lazy money into the jet fuel that "turbo-charged" his cash flow, helping him to rapidly pay down debt.

Next, get your line of credit and your checking account. The software determines exactly what you need; it's called a "line limit."

Before you can add money to your line of credit, you must have a balance due on it. This is where the software comes in. Based on the due dates of your debts and monthly household expenses, the software will instruct you to move money to your checking account from the line of credit to pay some monthly expenses. The software also specifies when to use the line of credit to make advanced principal payments on your consumer debts. This creates an outstanding balance on the line of credit.

When you receive your paycheck, deposit it into your checking account and then transfer the funds to the line of credit. This keeps the outstanding balance as low as possible. You're now leveraging the bank's low-interest line of credit to pay off your high-interest debt. It's a

> Leveraging the bank's low-interest line of credit to pay off your high-interest debt.

vital tool in the Mission ONE Million program, and we will show you how to leverage much more in the next chapter.

Financial leveraging is not a new concept. It's the ebb and flow that perpetuates trade. We believe, ultimately, it will bring a whole new perspective to the way people manage their cash flow and how they pay for things. We are on a mission to help America get out of debt, and this is one of the most effective ways to financially gain AND prosper.

Let's look at an actual client example. Mark gets paid $1,346 weekly; Sherry gets paid $1,923 every other week. After taxes, their net monthly income is close to $10,000. We entered those figures into the software along with their monthly household expenses (utilities, car insurance, phone, cable/internet, entertainment, etc.) as well as when they pay each bill.

We also entered their debts:

- Credit cards: one has a balance of $2,000 at 18 percent interest and the other has $5,000 at 13 percent
- An auto loan for $38,000 at 3.9 percent interest
- A student loan balance of $37,000 at 6 percent interest
- A thirty-year mortgage of $350,000 with a minimum payment of $2,071 and 4 percent interest.

The software uses algorithms, mathematical formulas that derive a desired result, that will factor in the utmost advantages of the line of credit. Sherry and Mark will be instructed **what** debt to pay, **when** to pay it, **how much** to pay, and **from where**. Not every month will be the same. Some months you may have to put new tires on the car or buy some new clothes for the family. Every time the expenses are adjusted, the program recalculates the client's situation. Its digital intelligence determines the most efficient way for you to use your own money—and the bank's money.

> Sherry and Mark will be instructed what debt to pay, when to pay it, how much to pay, and from where.

In this example, the couple netted roughly $10,000 in monthly income with $8,000 in expenses, leaving the software with $2,000 a month to work with. You don't have to have that much to use the system, but the higher the discretionary number, the faster debts can be eliminated.

The whole purpose of the software program is to accelerate the pay-off process. You aren't required to drastically alter your lifestyle. You are being more responsible with the discretionary funds you have available, and you are putting the unused portion of your paycheck to work, as opposed to spending it unwisely.

Let's go back to Sherry and Mark. We first ran their numbers in the fall of 2017. It was determined that they would be out of debt, including their mortgage if they so choose, in twelve years. But they don't have to wait that long to see results. Their first credit card was scheduled to be paid off in October of 2017. (It just happened that the card with the lowest balance, $2,000, had the highest interest rate.) The software is not concerned with interest rates because the idea is to pay the debt as quickly as possible. It attacks the lowest balance first, so you see results that keep you motivated.

If the couple creates more discretionary income, or someone gets a pay raise, or there's other money coming in, the software will adjust, and the credit cards will be paid off sooner.

Once the credit cards are paid off, the software focuses on the car loan. Because the money they were paying on the credit cards is now being used to pay off the car loan, it's scheduled to be paid off four years earlier.

The student loan will be paid off next, just a year and a half after the car is paid for, instead of the projected year, 2035. That's a huge savings!

Then, once all these consumer debts are paid off, Sherry and Mark will be able to redirect over $1,100 a month into their Wealth Builder account. This will allow them to enjoy life more and worry less about having enough money to pay bills every month, and they can start planning on a hopeful and prosperous financial future.

Oh, and they will have saved over $34,000 in interest, not to mention the savings of over $150,000 on the mortgage if they decide to pay that off. That's real opportunity.

When we ran these numbers through a financial calculator, they realized they could create an additional couple hundred thousand dollars for their retirement instead of spending their hard-earned money on interest. They were pretty happy.

Let's put your money to work—strategically, safely, and securely:

- 68 percent of Americans have little or no hope of getting out of debt.
- 71 percent are living paycheck to paycheck, even those who earn as much as $200,000 a year.

Until you master your cash flow, you cannot create wealth.

> ## Until you master your cash flow, you cannot create wealth.

Mastering your cash flow means practicing discipline, resisting instant gratification, and living within your means.

To do this requires some sacrifice. If you want to be slim, strong, and healthy, you must make wise choices when it comes to your physical health. Same goes for your financial health. If you want to be out of debt and creating wealth, you must make wise choices when it comes to spending and saving.

The cash-flow management software can accelerate the time it takes to get out of debt. It uses similar principles to the "snowball" effect—pay off the lowest balance debt first, then attack it on up the line. But because you're leveraging the bank's money you can even do it more quickly, saving you thousands of dollars in interest along the way.

As you get used to the new financial "you," there may be some detoxing along the way. It may hurt a little to put your new spending plan in place. A successful dieter (one who takes the weight off...and keeps it off) will tell you that it took a little bit of "oomph" to put the new plan in place, but it got easier the longer they stuck with it. The same holds for your finances. If you put yourself on a financial diet, the new way of spending will become *your* norm eventually, and you can bet you're going to feel happier. You are going to feel more in control of your life because your finances aren't dragging you down.

A good friend, Don Blanton, asks a very important question of his clients. If someone came to you and said, "Over the course of your lifetime, you're going to earn $2 million dollars. Instead of paying you a month at a time, I'm going to pay you the $2 million today. This will be all the money you will ever receive for the rest of your life." Would you spend the money any differently than the way you spend your money now?

We're betting you would. You would be more frugal, which means being thrifty, careful, or economical regarding money. We hope you would be diligent about protecting and saving it—with most of your money in a Wealth Builder interest-bearing account—so it would last the rest of your life.

The less money you spend on expenses, the more money you have to create wealth. We want your Wealth Builder account to be as full as it can be, so you can enjoy the fruits of your labor for many years to come.

We cannot stress this enough. Cash flow is your largest asset. How you manage your cash flow is going to determine your quality of your life, now and into the future. Instead of you doing what the majority of people do, we want you to become as financially independent as possible. Allocate your positive cash flow to create wealth. Stop allocating it towards depreciating assets and consumer debt. That's the heart of Mission ONE Million.

> **Allocate your positive cash flow to create wealth. Stop allocating it towards depreciating assets and consumer debt.**

It's impossible to know what you do not know. And lacking knowledge is very harmful. We want you to know your money's potential. There are things you've never been taught or you aren't even aware of. Keep reading. There is hope for a better now and a prosperous future.

THREE

How Money Works

ONLY 5 PERCENT OF AMERICANS USE THEIR MONEY COR-rectly. They're financially independent, meaning they have enough money to comfortably live the lifestyle they desire.

These are not necessarily wealthy people. The couple we told you about in the last chapter makes $10,000 a month. It can be done with less than that. It's not necessarily about how much money you make, it's about how you use the money you have.

> It's not necessarily about how much money you make, it's about how you use the money you have.

That's the key. But in order to use it, you need to know how money works. The 95 percent who are not financially independent are in poor shape because they've never been taught how to make money work to their advantage.

> The 95 percent who are not financially independent are in poor shape because they've never been taught how to make money work to their advantage.

If you're going to do all the hard work of eliminating your debt, you deserve to know the secrets of the financially independent. Besides, you want to know how to manage all the surplus cash you created from being debt free!

The secrets are really rules that financial institutions use all the time. Fortunately, these rules are not difficult to understand. When you apply them, you can grow your Wealth Builder account at a decent rate while protecting it from risk and unnecessary taxes. This allows you to take advantage of certain financial practices that banks use all the time. They make even more money with the money we think is sitting in their vaults.

Rule #1: Never Interrupt Compounding Interest

We know that interest is important. We want to pay the lowest interest rate we can on a loan or a credit card because we're paying less back to the lender over the course of the loan.

However, if we're earning interest on our money, say in a CD, a money-market account, or even a managed fund or stock market account, we want to earn the highest interest rate. This allows us to make the most on the money.

We are all familiar with the term "compounding interest." We love it because it's "interest on interest." This is when you're earning interest on both the principle and the interest you've already accrued, or made, on that money.

This simple chart demonstrates how compounding works based on an initial deposit of $100 with a static, or fixed, interest rate of 10 percent that compounds yearly:

	Principal	Interest earned
Initial Deposit – Year 1	$100	$10
New Principal – Year 2	$110	$11
New Principal – Year 3	$121	$12.10
New Principal – Year 4	$133.10	$13.31

You get the idea. Compounding interest makes your money grow faster than anything else. It's easy to see why Albert Einstein called it the eighth wonder of the world. It grows the $3,000 you saved (if you took our advice and brewed your own coffee and brought your lunch to work for a year) into $250,000 over the course of thirty years.

Almost all savings and investment vehicles use compounding interest for cash accumulation. It's an important rule to make sure you understand. But this "how money works in your favor" rule takes it one step further.

Compounding interest works best when it's *uninterrupted*. You want your money to grow continually. If it's interrupted because the market has a negative return, or loss, or you take money from your accounts, then the money you've made in previous years goes away. Your account balance is lowered, and you're not making as much interest.

> ## Compounding interest works best when it's *uninterrupted.*

In 2017, Dr. James came out to see us. We asked him how much money he lost in '08. He said it was just a "paper loss" when his account dropped from $600,000 to $300,000, and he knew it would recover to $600,000 again. That's true, but let's looks at what happened in the years from 2007 to 2017 to see how his account recovered:[2]

Compounding and Consistency are the Keys to Growth					
Year	Compounding ROR	Compounding EOY Balance	Speculation ROR	Speculation EOY Balance	Difference
2007	5.93%	$ 635,580	3.53%	$ 621,180	$ 14,400
2008	5.93%	$ 673,270	-38.49%	$ 382,088	$ 291,182
2009	5.93%	$ 713,195	23.45%	$ 471,687	$ 241,507
2010	5.93%	$ 755,487	12.78%	$ 531,969	$ 223,518
2011	5.93%	$ 800,288	0.00%	$ 531,969	$ 268,319
2012	5.93%	$ 847,745	13.41%	$ 603,306	$ 244,439
2013	5.93%	$ 898,016	29.60%	$ 781,885	$ 116,131
2014	5.93%	$ 951,268	11.39%	$ 870,941	$ 80,327
2015	5.93%	$ 1,007,679	-0.73%	$ 864,584	$ 143,095
2016	5.93%	$ 1,067,434	9.54%	$ 947,065	$ 120,369
2017	5.93%	$ 1,130,733	19.42%	$ 1,130,985	$ (252.00)

---

2 The speculative returns are based on the S&P 500 price only and do not include dividends.

Year one is 2007. He lost half his account value the following year. It took four years of the market performing exceptionally well for him to make up the difference.

This chart also illustrates another point, the difference between a predictable versus a speculative return. The average percentage of gains over these eleven years in the speculative market was 5.93 percent. This is a conservative return.

Wouldn't you rather have your money in a conservative predictable account as opposed to the nerve-racking ups and downs of the speculative stock market?

Here's how it looks in a line graph:

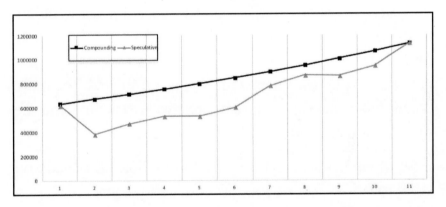

The uninterrupted compounding promotes steady, consistent growth. However, the stock market goes up and comes down.

The uninterrupted compounding promotes steady, consistent growth. However, the stock market goes up and comes down.

There are also other questions to consider. What would have happened if you were making an average of 7 percent instead? That would be $1,262,911 at the end of eleven years, a difference of over $130,000.

It is possible for the Wealth Builder account to average 7 percent. Which path would you prefer?

It's obviously the common-sense way to build wealth. It's consistent. You know your accumulation balance is going in the right direction, and it doesn't violate the next rule—

Rule #2: Never Put Your Capital at Risk

Basically, capital is your assets. The most important capital, to us, is the money you've accumulated in any savings or investment account. This is the sum of all the money you have put in, plus the interest that has accumulated. The more "capital" you have, the more interest you're earning and the more financially independent you become.

In other words, capital is the foundation on which you build cash flow. When you risk your capital, you are risking future cash flow.

> Capital is the foundation on which you build cash flow. When you risk your capital, you are risking future cash flow.

Your money is at risk when it's in the stock market. Still, many of us invest in the market anyway because we literally don't know any better. Many 401(k)s are in "managed funds"—which means they're in the stock market. IRA money (Individual Retirement Accounts) can be invested in the stock market or the bond market. Bond markets are often advertised as "safer" than the stock market, but they still are volatile, meaning you still risk losing your capital.

You got a peek at how the stock market works in the previous example. Here is another chart with an initial investment of $100,000, based on the S&P 500 returns since 2000:[3]

Year	Return %	Acct Value
2000	-10.14	$ 89,860
2001	-13.04	$ 78,142
2002	-23.37	$ 59,880
2003	26.38	$ 75,676
2004	8.99	$ 82,479
2005	3.00	$ 84,953
2006	13.62	$ 96,524
2007	3.53	$ 99,321
2008	-38.49	$ 61,468
2009	23.45	$ 75,882
2010	12.78	$ 85,580
2011	1.00	$ 86,436
2012	13.41	$ 98,027
2013	29.60	$ 127,043
2014	11.39	$ 141,513
2015	-0.73	$ 140,480
2016	9.54	$ 153,882
2017	19.42	$183,766
18 Yr Total	2.57%	$183,766

3   These returns represent the S&P 500 price only and do not include dividends. The S&P 500 is an unmanaged index that is generally considered representative of the U.S. stock market. The performance of an unmanaged index is not indicative of the performance of any particular investment. All S&P returns sourced at StandardandPoors.com.

We love the years when the stock market does well. Who doesn't like 29.6 percent gains? (That's what happened in 2013.) But look what happens when the market does poorly, like from 2000 to 2002, or in 2008, and even the slight loss in 2015?

This chart is based on an initial investment of $100,000. In the first three years of this millennia, this account lost a little over $40,000. From 2002 to 2007 the market rebounded. The account almost made it back to the $100,000 initial investment in 2007, but then 2008 happened. Disaster struck. The account lost almost all it had gained in less than nine months, because the market crashed in August of that year.

It took another five years (2009—2013) to finally get ahead of the initial $100,000 investment. That means out of the eighteen years that $100,000 was in the stock market, only five were showing positive gains on the initial investment. That's thirteen out of eighteen years that this account lost the opportunity of earning uninterrupted compounding interest. Most of the years, risk wreaked havoc on the account!

To make things even more uncomfortable, all these numbers assume that you've kept your money in the market for the long-haul and that you were invested in all the right stocks. If you had lower-performing stocks than what the S&P average showed, you would have lost more money. If you pulled your money out when the market crashed in '08 (which some people did), then you probably never recovered everything.

The 2008 crash was a decade ago, and many people don't remember the massive amount of pain that caused. We call this "financial amnesia." The stock market has done very well in the last ten years, and people have become somewhat complacent thinking they'll "get the (market) memo" before it crashes. That's what people thought in 1929.

The reality is the stock market is a roller coaster. Over the course of its history, it's gone up and down, and up and down. The last decade has enjoyed one of the longest-running bull markets in its history. (A "bull market" encourages buying as share prices are rising. In contrast, a "bear market" trends toward selling as share prices are dropping.) But here's the truth: Few can predict when the market will rise, dip… or crash, as it's constantly influenced by countless delicate variables. A market correction was projected in 2016. Instead, the market rebounded and made around a 12 percent return. That's great, but it isn't always going to be the case.

There is a ton of information out there about the stock market, but here's something to consider. Do you know enough about the stock market to feel comfortable risking your hard-earned money in it?

When you risk your money, you risk interrupting your compounded growth which, in turn, risks your future cash flow. When you don't risk your money, you don't have to worry about the downside of the stock market.

Most often a continuously compounding environment will produce better returns than the stock market over the long run, even when the stock market enjoys the high gains of recent years. That's what happens in the Wealth Builder account. When planned correctly, you will be more consistent and predictable, which allows you more financial freedom in the long-term.

> Most often a continuously compounding environment will produce better returns than the stock market over the long run.

Know Your Terms

The financial world is awash in investment lingo and difficult concepts. It's one of the reasons why most people don't understand how money works. Think about it. What is money after all? It's a symbol. It represents worth, and we must believe it's worth something for it to actually mean anything. Otherwise, that hundred dollar bill would just be a wrinkled piece of paper.

While it is not actually a rule, understanding certain financial terms is a vital component to controlling your financial health. There is a ton of vocabulary used in the world of money, and we've defined some already (words like "compounding" and "bull market"). We will continue to define terms as we move into the "Creating Wealth" section of the book. For now, know that the language used in stock-market investing is what confuses most people. When you're confused about how the stock market works, it becomes even riskier for your money. What you don't know really can hurt you.

We do encourage you to use the internet when you don't understand a financial term or word having to do with money. There are some very good sites that have easy-to-understand definitions. Understanding financial investment terms sets you on a clearer path and equips you to make better choices with your money.

> **Understanding financial investment terms sets you on a clearer path and equips you to make better choices with your money.**

There are only a few more terms to define in order for us to move forward. They have everything to do with you making sure your money is working in your favor and managing your cash flow well.

Returns: Average versus Actual Returns

A "return" is the money you make on your initial investment, either in interest rates like on CDs, Money Market accounts, or in stock market gains.

When you talk to a money manager or broker, you'll often hear about how their portfolios are earning a certain average percentage not an "actual" return. The "average" usually sounds pretty good. But what does it mean?

Here is a quick example to teach you the difference.

You started with $100.

By the end of the year, it grew 100 percent.

You now have $200.

But say the next year you lose 50 percent of that $200. You're back to $100.

What's your actual rate of return? Zero.

But your average rate of return would be 25 percent!

Here's how that works:

Year one you made 100 percent.

Year two you lost 50 percent. Subtract the 50 percent from the 100 percent and you have 50 percent.

Now divide that 50 percent by the investment period (two years) and your average rate of return is 25 percent.

Did you actually earn 25 percent? No, and that is the difference between average and actual rate of return.

The reality is an even bleaker picture.

What happens if you invest $100,000 in year one but the market dips 25 percent? Will you recover your money if the market recovers 25 percent the next year?

Unfortunately, no. While a loss of 25 percent and a gain of 25 percent mathematically creates an average of zero, when you lose 25 percent of your money in one year and gain 25 percent the next year, you've actually lost 6.25 percent of the original value of the money. Why? Because your account balance at the end of year one dropped by 25 percent. You started with a lower amount on which to make the next year's 25 percent.

The average rate of return of the S&P 500 price between 2000 and 2017 was 4.96 percent, but the actual rate of return during this period was 3.38 percent.

> **The average rate of return of the S&P 500 price between 2000 and 2017 was 4.96 percent, but the actual rate of return during this period was 3.38 percent.**

If you had invested $1 million in an S&P Index account in 2000, the following are the "average" versus the "actual" values of the account, based on price, ending in 2017:

- the *average* rate of return would produce $2,390,170
- the *actual* rate of return would produce $1,819,103.

That's a $571,066 difference! A lot of money by anyone's standards.

Sequence-of-Return Risks

We've already noted that many people have their 401(k)-money invested in the stock market. The risk factor alone is enough to turn us away from that strategy. But there's something else that happens when your money is invested in the market, and you're taking money out in retirement. It's something that puts it at even more risk.

As you can see from the average versus actual return scenario, when the market drops, say 10 percent in one year, you don't recover all your money if the market recovers 10 percent the next year. It takes 11.11 percent to recover the money you lost. So to make money, you would have to do better than the 11.11 percent.

If you are still working and flowing money into your savings, a market correction hurts, but it's not devastating.

But what happens if you're retired…and your retirement funds are in the stock market…and you're living on that money…and the market tanks?

You are not putting any additional money into the account. Instead, you're depleting it year by year, and you just lost more money because the market took a down turn.

This is called poor "sequence of returns" or "sequence of returns risk." It is what actually happens when you take money out of your equity account to live on and the market drops in value.

The "sequence" refers to when you take your money out of the market, because timing affects your returns.

Sequence-of-returns risk is what devastated so many retirement accounts in the crash of 2008. For example, let's say you retired in 2007, and you had all your retirement savings in the stock market. You decided to take a 4 percent distribution (that's what conventional wisdom teaches.[4]) Your stocks performed the same as the S&P 500: 3.53 percent. You just lost .47 percent of your retirement fund.

If you had $100,000 in your account to start, and took your distribution, your account would be slightly less than $100,000 at the end of the year. That's your starting balance at the beginning of 2008.

The market plummets in 2008. The S&P 500 showed a 38.49 percent loss. You still need to take your 4 percent distribution, so your account takes a double hit between the market loss and your distribution. That equals 42.49 percent. If you started with $100,000, you would have a balance of $57,000.

To get your money back to where you started, the market would have to perform at an unrealistic 74.76 percent the next year.

When the market tanks and you're taking distributions, the risk to your money is exponential.

When the market tanks and you're taking distributions, the risk to your money is exponential.

---

4   In recent years, many have questioned the validity of the 4 percent rule. The *Wall Street Journal* published an article entitled, "Say Goodbye to the 4% Rule," where they suggested a safe withdrawal rate to be only 2 percent. Kelly Greene. *WSJ*. https://www.wsj.com/articles/say-goodbye-to-the-4-rule-1376315815 3 Mar. 2013. Web. 28 Feb. 2018.

Arbitrage

We know. "Arbitrage" is a funny sounding word, and we don't use it in our day-to-day conversations. Yet, along with uninterrupted compounding, it's the most powerful financial concept we use to build wealth. Banks and other financial institutions create enormous wealth using arbitrage.

Simply put, arbitrage means borrowing money at a low rate of interest and earning money at a higher rate.

Banks make money by using "other people's money" (OPM) to earn a higher rate of return on it. In this case, OPM means yours and mine.

What would happen if you were able to use OPM and take advantage of arbitrage in your own Wealth-Building account? You guessed it—more capital, more wealth, and more financial freedom.

> What would happen if you were able to use OPM and take advantage of arbitrage in your own Wealth-Building account? You guessed it—more capital, more wealth, and more financial freedom.

You may have money in a Money Market account or in a savings account. You are earning interest—barely. Let's say you walk into the bank and deposit $10,000 or $20,000. You would earn what we call "point nothing," or less than one percent interest.

But what if you asked them for a car loan instead? The banks will likely quote you 3, 5, or maybe 6 percent interest on the loan. They tell you this is the cost of using "their" money (but we both know their money is really our money). If it's a credit card, the interest rate may be in the double digits.

> **The bank pays us, the depositors, less than one percent in many cases, and then loans us that SAME money at a much higher rate.**

The bank pays us, the depositors, less than one percent in many cases, and then loans us that SAME money at a much higher rate. In other words, the banks are borrowing money at a lower rate and are earning a higher rate. This is the epitome of "arbitrage."

Banks are very good at arbitrage, and they are wise to profit from its power. If I pay the bank 15 percent interest on a credit card that costs them less than 2 percent to maintain, then the bank is making money. The problem arises when you're likely "spending" that money, getting into more debt by using the credit card with the 15 percent interest.

This is how arbitrage works on a loan. Say you had a bucket of money with $10,000 in it, and it was earning 7 percent uninterrupted compounding interest. You were able to borrow against that bucket of money, and you were charged only 5 percent simple interest on the loan.

On the borrowed funds, the cost is $500 a year to use it. The accumulated money is growing at 7 percent interest and compounding on itself. Notice the difference between the paid interest and the earned interest in the following chart. The interest you're earning is more than the interest you're paying. That's arbitrage to your advantage—and it's so much wiser than paying the bank or credit card company 15 percent for the "privilege" of using "their" money.

Year	Paid Interest	Earned Intest	Account Value
1	$500	$ 700	$ 10,700
2	$500	$ 749	$ 11,449
3	$500	$ 801	$ 12,250
4	$500	$ 858	$ 13,108
5	$500	$ 918	$ 14,026
6	$500	$ 982	$ 15,007
7	$500	$ 1,051	$ 16,058
8	$500	$ 1,124	$ 17,182
9	$500	$ 1,203	$ 18,385
10	$500	$ 1,287	$ 19,672
11	$500	$ 1,377	$ 21,049
12	$500	$ 1,473	$ 22,522
13	$500	$ 1,577	$ 24,098
14	$500	$ 1,687	$ 25,785
15	$500	$ 1,805	$ 27,590
16	$500	$ 1,931	$ 29,522
17	$500	$ 2,067	$ 31,588
18	$500	$ 2,211	$ 33,799
19	$500	$ 2,366	$ 36,165
20	$500	$ 2,532	$ 38,697
21	$500	$ 2,709	$ 41,406
22	$500	$ 2,898	$ 44,304
23	$500	$ 3,101	$ 47,405

Instead of being constantly at a disadvantage, we'd be wise to mimic what banks are doing. We want everyone to be earning more interest than they are paying.

We often wonder why the concept of arbitrage isn't taught to our kids in school. It's one of those rules about money that if you learn it, and use it, your chances of becoming financially independent increase almost to a certainty.

We often wonder why the concept of arbitrage isn't taught to our kids in school. It's one of those rules about money that if you learn it, and use it, your chances of becoming financially independent increase almost to a certainty.

■ ■ ■

We want you to win at the game of money. If you don't know the rules, you don't have a chance. You'll be swallowed up by those that do, and you'll stay in the 95 percentile—those who don't know how to manage their cash flow pay a high price for the privilege of using their own money.

We created Mission ONE Million because we're done watching others struggle. We want you to learn more so your best asset, your cash flow, is never compromised. Now that you know some of the basic rules, we're going to show you how you can use them in tandem with your other main assets—your mortgage, 401(k)s or other qualified plans, and your non-qualified money you may have in the stock market.

This will set you up for success. You deserve it.

—FOUR—

Doin' Your Money Right Part One: Qualified and Non-Qualified Money

I T REALLY IS ALL ABOUT MANAGING CASH FLOW.
Having bad debt, putting your money at risk, and paying more interest than what you earn, are all detrimental to your cash flow.

Earning uninterrupted compounding in a "true compounding" environment where your capital is protected puts you in control of your cash flow. You can effectively manage your cash flow so that you always have income, no matter if you're working, on vacation, or retired.

There are several valid ways to handle your money—and it's important to know they all have pros and cons. However, we choose to lead by example and manage our cash flow using the principles we just talked about.

We know from experience that when you follow these rules, you get the intended result: cash flow, managed in such a way that it will never run out.

> We know from experience that when you follow these rules, you get the intended result: cash flow, managed in such a way that it will never run out.

According to a 2016 article in Money, one in three Americans have zero saved for retirement, and 23 percent of Americans have $10,000 or less.[5]

In the same year, a Forbes article reported that "more Americans are participating in retirement plans today than ever before. Total retirement plan contributions are rising, and employers are contributing more to retirement plans." [6]

Either extreme warrants the BEST plan for retirement, the Wealth Builder account, but the popular choice is a qualified plan.

People ask us all the time, "What's a qualified plan?" It's yet another money concept not fully understood.

If you have a 401(k) plan through your employer, you have a qualified plan. It's a retirement plan established by

---

5   "One in Three American Has Saved $0 for Retirement." Money. Mar 14, 2016. http://time.com/money/4258451/retirement-savings-survey/. Accessed 01 Mar, 2018.

6   Andrew Biggs. "Why Retirees Aren't Running Out of Money." Forbes. https://www.forbes.com/sites/andrewbiggs/2016/07/14/retirees-arent-running-out-of-money-but-why/#45aaa3b43853. July 14, 2016.

your employer as a way to save for your retirement. The term "qualified" means the amount deducted from your paycheck and contributed to your 401(k) is tax deferred. In other words, you're postponing the income tax on the contribution until you take retirement distributions.

It's important for you to know how qualified plans work, so you can decide if it's the best way to handle your money.

Qualified plans were set up by Congress and the IRS when employers were no longer able—or willing—to offer pensions to their tenured employees.

It used to be, our parents (or grandparents) could work for a major corporation, like IBM or General Electric, for twenty-five to thirty years or longer. After serving their time, they were eligible to be vested in a pension. It was a retirement paycheck for the rest of their life based upon their income, years of service, and the organization they worked for. In some cases, if they passed away, their spouse may have gotten a part of the pension, but their children wouldn't receive anything.

Pensions were meant to attract and keep employees who wanted to work for the same company or corporation for their entire working life. But the employee's retirement was pretty much out of their hands. To earn a better retirement meant they had to work longer, get a promotion or a raise, or live longer. The employer controlled how much they funded their pensions and where they were investing them.

The 1970s brought to America disco and staggering inflation. People were living longer, and it was becoming increasingly difficult for companies to pay all those pensions.

I guess you could say the pensions were taking a toll on the company store—for twenty to thirty years after the employee left the company!

High inflation and pension funds running out of money prompted legislation that changed retirement forever. It went from being the responsibility of the employer to the employee shouldering most of the burden. It was 1978, and the "defined contribution plan," or qualified plan was born. Employees were able to contribute part of their income, tax-deferred.

This means that you don't pay income tax on the portion of your paycheck that goes to the 401(k). You do get taxed on it when you take the money out, and there are the rules—you can't access it until you're 59 ½ without paying a penalty and you must start taking distributions when you're 70 ½, or pay a penalty.

The employer could also contribute, but they weren't on the hook for making sure they (the employer) had saved enough for the employee. They wanted you, the employee, to be mostly responsible for your retirement and not them, the employer.

There are a number of different qualified plans depending on the type of work you do: 401(k)s, TSPs, SEPs, and 403(b)s to name a few.

IRAs (Individual Retirement Accounts) are also tax-deferred accounts, and while they act just like a qualified plan, they technically are not. They are meant to supplement retirement income, and they were created four years before the "qualified plans."

There is a lot of fuss over whether you should have a qualified plan like the 401(k) and whether you should "max fund" it (meaning putting in as much money as you're allowed to by the IRS) or only put in the amount your employer is going to match.

The simplicity for us is your 401(k) should follow these rules:

1. Never interrupt compounding
2. Always protect your capital

The best way to handle a qualified plan requires a look at two issues: how the 401(k) is being invested and what are the real consequences of money being "tax deferred."

We noted earlier that many 401(k) plans are invested in the stock market in some way. They're usually in a "diversified" portfolio that includes mutual funds and bonds. Money Market investments are also used, but they fall under the "point zero" issue we discussed in the previous chapter (meaning Money Market accounts usually earn around 1 percent, or "1 point" of interest. Not enough to retire on, for sure).

If your money is invested in the stock market, it is at risk. This means that if the market dips or crashes, your compounding interest is interrupted, you've lost the opportunity to make money on the money lost. Your capital is not protected, and thus a 401(k) that's invested in the stock market does not follow our rules.

Tax-Deferred

The issue of "tax deferred" is a little more complicated.

It sounds pretty darn good. Who likes to pay taxes? The idea behind the 401(k) is that you save money. You are not taxed on that income when it's taken out of your paycheck. The idea is that when you are retired, you're not making as much income so your tax bracket is supposed to be lower. This would work great if, and only if, the tax brackets stayed stable.

They don't.

- The highest tax bracket was 94 percent in the 1940s and remained high at 70 percent during the 1950s, 60s, and 70s.
- During Ronald Regan's term in office, the top tax bracket dropped to 28 percent.
- During the 1990s, the rate jumped to 39.6 percent, dropped to 35 percent, and stayed there until 2012.
- In 2012, the Obama administration passed The Patient Protection and Affordable Care Act, and the top tax rates jumped to 43.4 percent.[7]
- Just recently, the Trump "Tax Cuts and Jobs Act" cut the top income tax rate to 37 percent.

Tax rates rise and fall, and there is no guarantee that the tax deduction you're getting in your qualified plan now is going to be the tax rate you'll be paying on the distributions when you retire.

---

7   https://bradfordtaxinstitute.com/Free_Resources/Federal-Income-Tax-Rates.aspx

Here's how we look at these tax rates in terms of qualified plans:

Conventional wisdom says if you're putting money away in your qualified plan and it would be taxed at a higher rate than what you will pay when you get it out, then it's a good thing.

If you put your money in when the tax brackets were low and you had to take the money when tax brackets were raised again, then it's a bad thing.

We all know how badly the government is in debt. What are the chances of taxes being higher down the road to pay for all that debt? It's not a chance we're comfortable taking.

Let's look at it this way.

What if, over the last twenty years, you saved a million dollars in your 401(k) and you were in the top bracket. Let's make it 40 percent so you can easily see what we mean here.

That means that you did not have to pay $400,000 in income taxes on the million dollars.

But taxes drop drastically, and you are now in a lower 20 percent tax bracket.

Should you take out the million dollars and pay the 20 percent income tax, or leave it in and hope the government doesn't raise taxes again?

We would suggest you strategically start rolling the money out and pay the lower tax rate—because that would be a big win, saving 20 percent on taxes on that much money.

This is why we say, if you're putting your money in a qualified plan when taxes are 40 percent, and you take it out at 20 percent, it's a great deal.

But if you're putting it in at 20 percent and taking it out at 40 percent, that is a very expensive plan.

We have always advocated that you use a 401(k) if your employer is matching funds. That's like free money. But don't put in any more than that. Most important, always make sure your money is in a place where the capital is protected. If the stock market tanks, whatever tax advantage you had becomes a moot point. You've lost your money, and as we pointed out in the last chapter, it's not a "paper loss." It's lost opportunity because whatever you lost in the stock market dip is no longer in your account earning interest.

We think that putting in more money in a 401(k) plan beyond what the employer is matching is not the best use of your savings. It is much safer in the Wealth Builder account.

Go back and look at your qualified plan. What tax bracket were you in when you put the money in? What's your tax bracket now? If it's lower, then it's time to consider a strategic roll out.

Non-qualified Money

Most of the money we put away in savings falls under the category of "non-qualified." This is money on which we pay income tax when we earn it, and we can do with it what we please.

One option is to stick non-qualified money in CD's or Money Market accounts. CD rates are running at around 2.5 percent interest; Money Markets, 1.5 percent. This is, again, what Steve calls, "point nothing," and the money made in interest is taxed yearly, so it's basically making nothing. Factor in inflation and often times CDs and Money Market earnings are negative. The spending power of your money is less, so if you're making nothing on your savings, and you can't buy as much with it when you take it out, you have negative gains.

Non-qualified money can be put in the stock market. This is what most people do. But that is risky, and that violates our rules. No one knows when the market is going to nose dive. That and you are paying fees on that account—fees you may or may not know about.

Non-qualified money is far better off in an account that accumulates non-interrupted compounded interest without risk. If there are tax advantages to that account, even better.

Mission ONE Million is about creating wealth. We want one million people saving money, which will flip the percentage of Americans who are prepared for retirement. We don't want anyone to suffer financially, not when they're working and certainly not in their golden years, because they didn't manage their money according to the rules we just gave.

Follow the rules of how money works, and you truly win.

—FIVE—

Doin' Your Money Right Part Two: Your Mortgage

W E USUALLY THINK OF OUR HOUSE AS AN ASSET AND the mortgage as the liability. The home has equity; the mortgage is debt.

It's also conventional wisdom to pay off your mortgage early. There's a historical reason for that. Early mortgages were tough. You had to pay upwards of 50 percent down, you paid interest only for five years and at the end of that, you had to pay off the principal—the dreaded "balloon payment." If you didn't pay, the bank took your home. To protect ourselves from foreclosure, we think, "Pay it off." If you own it, it's yours.

But if you don't have a mortgage anymore, you still have to pay property taxes, homeowners insurance, and maintenance costs. You also lose a valuable mortgage interest deduction on your income tax.

Remember in chapter 2 when we talked about good debt and bad debt? Bad debt eats you up in interest. Good debt allows you to deduct interest from your income taxes.

If you have a $215,000 thirty-year mortgage, and you pay 4 percent in interest, your monthly payment is around $1,000. Each year you pay on your mortgage, you get to deduct about $9,000 in interest from your income.

Oftentimes, that's the difference between paying income taxes or getting a refund. That's good debt. Mortgages play a vital role in your monthly cash flow. Paying off your mortgage, we believe, is detrimental—sometimes highly so—to your cash flow.

A properly designed mortgage can create a big advantage to your cash flow; it can help you build wealth, interestingly enough. But if you misuse it, it will do the exact opposite— consume your wealth and even potentially cause more debt.

Mortgage ReFi is NOT an ATM

The *Wall Street Journal* in 2017 reported that nearly 50 percent of the mortgage loans last year were cash-out refinances.[8]

People have been taking the money out of the equity of their homes in cash. In other words, they are treating their equity like an ATM. If they were using that money to build

---

8   Cash-Out Option Hot Again with Home Refinancers. May 30, 2017. Wall Street Journal podcast. http://www.wsj.com/podcasts/cash-out-option-hot-again-with-home-re-financers/65D6BC7D-8771-42D3-8528-7385B05F5DEE.html.

wealth in the Wealth Builder account, then it's not a bad thing. However, for most that isn't happening.

The average mortgage balance across the country is about $223,000. The average mortgage payment is $1,000. People refinance their mortgage on average every five years. The house appreciates in value as the debt is reduced, and people see this as a way to pay for their kid's college, go on a vacation, or just buy something they want. That's not a good use of the money.

Some people take the equity and pay off accumulated debt which is smart, but then they don't know what to do with the surplus cash, so they squander the increased cash flow; they increase their lifestyle spending. This is why people in retirement end up with twenty-five years left on their mortgage, a lot of debt, and not enough savings to see them through.

What Happens When You Pay Off Your Mortgage

We realize that saying "paying off your mortgage is a big mistake," is controversial. Some folks are determined to get their house paid off no matter what.

A couple years ago, a seventy-year-old man came to see us. His house was worth about $400,000, and he had it completely paid for. He had waited until age seventy to claim his Social Security; his wife was a little bit younger than he was, and she had already claimed her benefit.

Sounds like they had done everything right. But the problem was they only had about $11,000 saved to sustain them during their retirement years. They were house-rich and cash-poor.

They still had to pay property taxes, income taxes, and maintenance costs. If they needed long-term care or found themselves not able to pay their bills, they would either have to sell their house or take out a reverse mortgage.

The point is, he should have built wealth first and dealt with his mortgage last.

For example, if this seventy-year-old had squirreled away the $400,000 into a Wealth Builder account earning an average of 7 percent per year, instead of putting all that money into his house, he would be earning about $28,000 per year in interest from the $400k.

The mortgage payment on a $400,000 home loan could be as low as $12,800 per year in today's financial environment.

So instead of being house rich and cash poor, he would have a positive cash flow of over $15,000 per year.

By not paying off his house, this retiree would have more per year in cash flow than he saved over a life time in his supplemental retirement savings account. This is an example of positive arbitrage and never interrupting compounding, and this chart illustrates that point:

Mortgage	Interest Rate	Tax Rate	Earned Int. Rate
$400,000	4.00%	20.00%	7.00%
Yr	Paid Interest	Earned Interest	Wealth Builder
1	$12,800	$ 28,000	$ 428,000
2	$12,800	$ 29,960	$ 457,960
3	$12,800	$ 32,057	$ 490,017
4	$12,800	$ 34,301	$ 524,318
5	$12,800	$ 36,702	$ 561,021
6	$12,800	$ 39,271	$ 600,292
7	$12,800	$ 42,020	$ 642,313
8	$12,800	$ 44,962	$ 687,274
9	$12,800	$ 48,109	$ 735,384
10	$12,800	$ 51,477	$ 786,861
11	$12,800	$ 55,080	$ 841,941
12	$12,800	$ 58,936	$ 900,877
13	$12,800	$ 63,061	$ 963,938
14	$12,800	$ 67,476	$ 1,031,414
15	$12,800	$ 72,199	$ 1,103,613
16	$12,800	$ 77,253	$ 1,180,865
17	$12,800	$ 82,661	$ 1,263,526
18	$12,800	$ 88,447	$ 1,351,973
19	$12,800	$ 94,638	$ 1,446,611
20	$12,800	$ 101,263	$ 1,547,874

The Windfall

What if you were to receive a windfall of money? (Maybe you got an inheritance or even won the lottery. It happens.)

We had a lady visit us who had a $250,000 house with a principal payment of $1,194 a month. Her interest rate was 4 percent. She received an inheritance large enough to be able to pay the house off.

That might be all well and good, but what happens then? She doesn't have that large amount of money accessible or working for her. Remember the rules of smart money management: Protect your capital and never interrupt compounding.

> If she pays off her house, she no longer has a mortgage payment, but she also no longer has control of the capital.

If she pays off her house, she no longer has a mortgage payment, but she also no longer has control of the capital.

If the capital is stuck in the bricks and mortar of the house, Rule #1 is broken: she interrupted compounding interest.

What happens if her house drops in value? She loses the value and control of the capital. Rule #2 broken. The capital is no longer protected.

This woman decided to keep her mortgage. Why? Because of the math. We showed her how she could take the windfall of funds and put the $250,000 immediately to work in her Wealth Builder account, earning uninterrupted compounding interest and protecting the capital.

If the Wealth Builder account earned an average of 7 percent interest, over the next thirty years she would profit $1.4 million. This accounts for paying the bank back their money with interest for the house, which would be $250,000 for the house and $240,000 in interest for a total of $490,000.

Remember arbitrage: you borrow low and earn a higher rate of interest. In this case, this woman held a mortgage at 4 percent interest, but could earn an average of 7 percent in her Wealth Builder account. If her money was tied up in the house, she wouldn't have been able to take full advantage of those gains.

Is Your Home the Right Fit?

One of the biggest mistakes homebuyers make is the size of the house they purchase.

For example, if you buy too big a house, it jams up your cash flow. Even if everything seems to be going along perfectly, as soon as there is one glitch, you get over extended. Between helping the kids with college or the car breaking down unexpectedly, things become too tight. You also can't invest because all your money is tied up in the house.

When you retire, you may not be able to afford the larger house payment. If times are good, maybe you can sell the real estate and hopefully it has appreciated. But as we found out in '08, home values don't always go up and the equity in your home is not always liquid—meaning you can't access it when you need it.

Or what happens if you retire, and you don't have your mortgage deduction? You're drawing on your 401(k), paying income tax on the distribution, but you don't have the cushion of the mortgage deduction.

Part of the Mission ONE Million strategy is to get your mortgage, one of your biggest expenses, working in your favor. If you start defaulting on your mortgage, you might end up losing your house altogether. You could land in bankruptcy. Neither scenario is good for your financial health.

> Part of the Mission ONE Million strategy is to get your mortgage, one of your biggest expenses, working in your favor.

We would love if every financial services professional, mortgage planner, and real estate agent worked to sell you the right house for you so that you build equity, have a life, and still invest for the future. Isn't *that* the American dream?

The Educated Refi

The interest you pay affects your cash flow. As we write this in 2018, we have seen historically low interest rates continue for ten years, but we are seeing rates beginning to rise on mortgages. If that happens, and you aren't proactive, you are going to find that not only are you going to add hundreds of dollars more to the payment, you are going to add tens of thousands of dollars in interest to the loan.

If you have a $300,000 mortgage with a 4 percent interest rate, your mortgage payment (excluding escrows) would be around $1,432 per month.

Most people don't realize that a mortgage is front-loaded on the interest payment. You are paying mostly interest up front; it is not until about the twenty-first year that you really begin making substantial principal payments. The payment stays the same each month, but the amount of principal and interest you pay each month varies. Over time you will have paid over $215,000 in interest on that original $300,000.

If interest rates go back up to 5 percent, that $1,432 monthly payment increases to over $1,600 and the total interest paid jumps to almost $280,000.

What happens if we start seeing 6 percent interest rates again? If the economy continues to heal, that's what will happen. We know it sounds counterintuitive, but when the economy is weak, interest rates stay low.[9] You'll not only be paying $300 to $400 more a month, but also pay more in interest (at just under $350,000) than the amount of the mortgage.

We began this chapter by talking about the wrong reason why people refinance their home. Refinancing to a lower interest rate is smart. Using the money from the refinance as an "ATM," however, will not lead to financial independence. Quite the opposite will happen.

However, there is a very smart way to use a refinance. As we write this, you may be able to get the lower interest rate, and you can use the cash to build wealth. We call it an "educated refinance."

---

9   Jeff Cox. "Fed's Fischer: Weak economy keeping interest rates low. https://www.cnbc.com/2017/07/31/feds-fischer-weak-economy-is-keeping-interest-rates- low.html.

Let's say a couple has a home valued at $375,000 and they owe $250,000. The $125,000 difference between what their home is worth and what they owe is their equity (assuming they can refinance or sell it for that price).

Let's say they have $1,000 tied up in debt payments:

> $450 car payment for a $20,000 car loan at 4 percent interest for 48 months and $580 in credit card payments for $13,000 worth of debt at 8 percent interest.

It could take many years to pay all that off. Is there a better way?

An educated refinance, which we also call the "mortgage-master move," works like this:

1. Refinance the home
2. Use the cash to pay off bad debt. In other words, roll the bad debt into the mortgage, which is good debt.
3. The debt isn't eliminated; it's transferred to debt with better terms, and the interest is tax-deductible. This also frees up cash flow.
4. If there is surplus from the refi, put some of it in the Wealth Builder account where it's earning uninterrupted compounding interest in a protected environment.
5. Use the increased cash flow wisely. Use some for lifestyle, but put away most of it into the Wealth Builder account.

> ## Use the increased cash flow wisely.
> ## Use some for lifestyle, but put away most of it
> ## into the Wealth Builder account.

6. In this case, let's say this educated refinance freed-up $1,000 a month for this couple. What most people would do is take that money, put it in their pocket, and increase their lifestyle. They might have a somewhat better life now, but they've really just kicked the can down the road and extended the mortgage another five or six years. Not good.

    But what if that couple took that same $1,000 a month and put it in a Wealth Builder account which averaged 7 percent interest compounded yearly? At the end of fifteen years, they would have $322,657 saved. That would be enough to pay off the balance on the house (at this point, around $137,000) and still have about $183,000 left.

Now, remember, if this couple chooses to pay off their mortgage, they lose their tax deduction. They're also leaving themselves open to financial hardship. If housing prices drop or if they need the cash, it's tied up in the equity of the house and not easily accessible.

The couple we've been talking about in this example were forty-six when they did their refinance. Most banks would have done the refinance without advising them to do something positive with the money. Worse, they would not be scheduled to pay off their mortgage until they were seventy-six years old.

Because they chose to do the educated refinance and put the surplus in the Wealth Builder for the next twenty-odd years, they set themselves up to take around $45,000 a year in income for the rest of their lives. Plus, because of the Wealth Builder's special tax privileges, they can take out the income tax-free. (We will cover that point in the next few chapters.)

With an educated refinance, their cash is now liquid, and their Wealth Builder account is building a nice income stream for themselves in the future.

The Fifteen versus Thirty-Year Mortgage

Most people have a thirty-year mortgage, but it's been the latest "rage" to get a fifteen-year mortgage. There is only one reason why you would get a fifteen-year mortgage—pay off your house faster.

> If you're paying more for your mortgage, you have less cash flow.

We have covered why that is not a good idea in a number of different places. If you're paying more for your mortgage, you have less cash flow. If you pay your house off early, that's great, but you risk being in the "house rich /cash poor" group. Either way, you reduce your ability to earn uninterrupted compounded interest, and you are putting your equity (which is part of your capital) at risk. Your cash flow is hindered. This violates the rules for smart money management.

Let's look at the difference between the payments of a $300,000 mortgage amortized over fifteen year's verses thirty years. I will use a 3.5 percent interest rate for the fifteen-year mortgage verses 4.25 percent rate for the thirty-year mortgage (because the interest rates for a fifteen-year mortgage are usually lower than a thirty-year):

- the fifteen-year mortgage payment is $2,144
- the thirty-year mortgage payment is $1,475
- the difference is $669.

That is $669 dollars a month you would *not* have available to build wealth if you're in a fifteen-year mortgage. On the flip side, that's $669 you could be putting away every month into your Wealth Builder account.

If you would put this difference of $669 per month in Wealth Builder account earning 7 percent after fifteen years you would have accumulated $216,000 dollars. The balance on the thirty-year mortgage in the fifteenth year would be $195,400. So, if you paid the exact dollar amount you would pay for a fifteen-year mortgage on the thirty-year, and you put away the difference, you would not only have enough to pay off the mortgage if you so choose, but you would save $20,600 in the process.

Here's a real-life example of how this works:

A couple came in about eight years ago. They were in their fifties at the time. Their kids were grown and out of the house. They made good income (over $200,000 a year), but they had accumulated some debt. We have found over the years that the larger your income, typically the more debts and expenses you have.

This couple had $6,500 in credit card debt and a car loan for $56,000. The credit cards were manageable; the car loan was a bit high. Their house was worth about $675,000, well above the average home loan amount. In this case, they did have adequate equity to do a refi.

The last refinance they did was for a fifteen-year mortgage. We're not sure why. It wasn't going to be there "forever house," meaning they weren't going to live out their retirement there.

We showed them how they could use a thirty-year mortgage more effectively, still have enough in their Wealth Builder account to pay off the house in fifteen years, and their money would still be available. They agreed to what we proposed, and this is what happened.

We sent them to our local mortgage professional. He reminded them that a cash-out refinance needed to be treated with respect and put them in a thirty-year mortgage. This allowed them to pay off their bad debt which freed up about $3,000 a month.

Because we got rid of all of the other debt, all they had left was the mortgage. That payment went up by about $150 a month, but we had canceled out $3,000 of other monthly payments, so they were left with $2,850 a month. They could either use that towards extra principal payments or put it in a Wealth Builder account.

They had been putting $1,000 a month into their respective 401(k)s at work. When we asked them if they thought they were going to have enough money saved for the future (they had several hundred thousand dollars). They didn't think they were on the course they needed to be.

The couple decided to use $600 of their freed-up cash flow for lifestyle spending. They put the remaining $2,250 into a Wealth Builder account, double what they were putting away in their 401(k)s.

Assuming a 7 percent average growth rate, we estimated that they would have over $950,000 in about seventeen years from their start date. Fast forward eight years. The gentleman recently told us that he is now planning to work a little longer than originally expected. Three more years of contributions and compounding interest will grow that account up to $1,263,317.

Who knows how much they'll have in their 401(k)s? That money is in the stock market...subject to risk. We have one shot at doin' money right. This isn't about freeing up frivolous party money; it's ensuring a quality of life for the future.

Who knows how much they'll have in their 401(k)s? That money is in the stock market. . .subject to risk. We have one shot at doin' money right.

An additional $1.2 million for retirement will give this couple much more peace of mind. Their lifestyle can be more secure. But they also know that if they need money for an emergency, they can access their Wealth Builder account instead of racking up credit card bills.

> Be smart with your mortgage by following the mortgage-master move to create wealth.

We want you to be smart and use every opportunity! Be smart with your mortgage by following the mortgage-master move to create wealth. You can have far more command over your cash flow. You can put your money in a place where it's growing steadily yet not subject to risk. Don't wait on the IRS or the federal government to do your money right. You can use your money when you want it.

Why would you do anything different?

SIX

The Wealth Builder Account: What Is It?

M OST PEOPLE HAVE A PREFERRED PLACE TO PUT THEIR money. It almost always includes the following benefits:

- Decent rate of return
- No risk of exposure
- Minimal taxes, if any, on the gains
- Liquidity, or access at any time
- No restrictions on access/distribution
- No limits on contributions
- Contributions are tax-deductible

The Wealth Builder account provides all of these benefits, except contributions are not tax deductible. We have made it very clear. When it comes to creating wealth, the financial rules we must follow are:

- Always enjoy uninterrupted compounding
- Never put capital at risk
- Protect and grow capital so it creates a positive cash flow.

The Wealth Builder account obeys all the rules of smart money management. It's the standard to which we refer in each scenario, example, and chart—and it's a life insurance policy.

> The Wealth Builder account obeys all the rules of smart money management. It's the standard to which we refer in each scenario, example, and chart—and it's a life insurance policy.

You may be rolling your eyes or blurting out, *"Life insurance! Are you kidding?! That's an expense, not an asset. It's money I'm spending to comfort and support my family when I die."*

Life insurance is often called "death insurance." It's what your grandfather purchased to make sure your grandmother had money to live on when he died. It still exists today; it's called "term insurance." A minimal amount is paid for a specific amount of death benefit, which the beneficiary receives upon the policy owner's death. This type of policy is not designed to grow money, and once the years of the "term" are up, the policy ends.

There's nothing to show for the cost of keeping the policy in force—except the comfort in knowing that, if the policy owner had died, a benefit would have been paid to the beneficiary.

That's not the kind of life insurance we're talking about here.

It's not "Whole Life" either. Whole Life insurance provides some of the same benefits as the life insurance we use for the Wealth Builder account, but it has a few disadvantages. Mainly, it cannot grow wealth as efficiently or as quickly, the earnings on the cash value are lower, and it typically is more expensive to own.

The type of life insurance that we use to build wealth is a newer type of life insurance. It's called *Indexed Universal Life Insurance,* or IUL for short.

> The type of life insurance that we use to build wealth is a newer type of life insurance.

Just like the cash-flow accumulation software is the twenty-first century tool to handle debt, the IUL is its equivalent to successfully and safely creating wealth.

Life Insurance 101

In order for Life Insurance to be classified by the IRS as "life insurance," and not an investment, it must have a death benefit attached to it.

The death benefit is important for two reasons:

1. Normally it pays a big financial benefit to the beneficiary when the policy owner passes away. Every time we deliver a death-benefit to someone who has lost a loved one, the relief a financial

benefit provides is palpable. It reminds us of one of the reasons we do what we do.

2.   The size of the death benefit dictates the wealth-creating properties of the IUL. The latter comes from the premiums that are allowed to be paid into the policy. The premiums are the foundation of the "cash value."

The "cash value" is what creates wealth. In the IUL policy, it is the

- total of your premiums paid
- plus the interest earned
- minus the cost of the death benefit.

> ## The premiums are the foundation of the "cash value."

You may have noticed "minus the cost," in the list above. Any financial vehicle that pays interest has a cost. Insurance is no exception, and we will show you how the cost of the IUL works in the next chapter. You might be surprised to learn these costs are normally not as expensive as management fees for most managed investment accounts.

Cash value is the money that is earning interest in the IUL. It can earn interest in one of two ways, a fixed interest account or an equity index account:

1.   In a fixed interest account the interest is "fixed" for that year, meaning the interest you earn doesn't change. No matter what happens in the financial world during that year, the cash value

is protected from loss and guaranteed to earn the fixed rate for that year. Fixed interest offers a very safe environment for your money.

The current fixed-rate of interest for the IUL is between 4 to 5 percent. With this option, your cash value can earn a fixed rate of return compounding each year for the life of the policy. You can build predictable wealth this way.

2. The other way you can earn interest in an Index Universal Life policy is through an equity index allocation. This is why it's called "Index Universal Life."

"Indexing" means that your money is linked to the growth of an equity index, allowing the IUL to participate in stock market-linked gains without the stock market risk. This is because your money isn't actually in the stock market.

> "Indexing" means that your money is linked to the growth of an equity index, allowing the IUL to participate in stock market-linked gains without the stock market risk. This is because your money isn't actually in the stock market.

"Indexing" is a way to enjoy the upside potential of the stock market while being protected from the loss.

When your money is in an "index" account, it's tied (or linked) to one of the stock market indices, like the Standard and Poor's 500, (S&P 500). The Dow Jones Industrial is another very familiar index. It's actually the oldest stock index and was created by Charles Dow, the founder of The Wall Street Journal.[10]

These indices measure the average performance of a number of designated stocks at any given time on any given day the stock market is open. The S&P 500 measures five hundred of America's largest corporations based on profit. The Dow measures a set of thirty public companies in the U.S., all of them are "blue chip"—financially fit companies with dependable performance, such as General Electric and Walt Disney.

A stock market index measures the price change of the specified group of stocks. When you hear, "The S&P jumped ten points today," that means the value of the stocks in that index went up that day by a certain percentage amount; however, the current level of the index has no dollar value correlation. How those points are figured is complicated and based on the value of the stocks and the percentage of increase or decrease.

What's important, here, is the insurance companies use the value of the index to calculate the amount of interest they credit your account for that year. The cash value of your policy is not participating in the market. The insurance company does not invest your money in any stock or bond.

---

10   "What's the Difference between the Dow Jones Industrial and the S&P 500?" http://www.investopedia.com/ask/answers/130.asp.

> The cash value of your policy is not participating in the market. The insurance company does not invest your money in any stock or bond.

You might be asking yourself, "Even though my money isn't in the market, wouldn't it still be exposed to risk because the interest is tied to stock market index returns?"

That's a good question. It has to do with two provisions in the indexing crediting mechanism of an IUL policy—the cap and the floor.

- The cap determines the participation percentage in market-linked returns.
- The floor is the mechanism that guarantees no losses, keeping money in a true compounding environment.

The Safety Net

The "floor" is a safety net built into the indexing portion of an IUL. It is set by contract, usually at 0 percent. This means that if the index falls below the contracted amount (the 0 percent) the cash value is protected.

In other words, the cash value will never suffer a negative rate of return. If the stock market dips, tanks, or even plummets, the value of the cash is not lost.

Let's say the index you choose to link your cash to each year is the S&P 500 index. It dips negative 10 percent like it did in 2000. Did you lose money? No. Your floor was set at 0 percent; your cash value doesn't participate in the market loss. Your account doesn't earn any interest that year, but if you had the choice of making zero on your money or losing money in 2000, or worse, in 2008, which would you choose? Pretty much everyone I talk to chooses zero earnings over loss, every time.

The floor in an IUL is a protective and conservative feature.

It ensures that you never interrupt compounding.

Take a closer look at the following chart we showed you in chapter 3. Again, it's based on the returns in the S&P 500 index with an initial investment of $100,000:[11]

Starting Account Value $100,000		
Year	Return%	Account Value
2007	3.53%	$ 103,530
2008	-38.49%	$ 63,681
2009	23.45%	$ 78,614
2010	12.78%	$ 88,661
2011	1.00%	$ 89,548
2012	13.41%	$ 101,556
2013	29.60%	$ 131,617
2014	11.39%	$ 146,608
2015	-0.73%	$ 145,538
2016	9.54%	$ 159,422
2017	19.42%	$ 190,382
11 Yr Tot	6.03%	$ 190,382

11 These returns represent the S&P 500 price only and do not include dividends. The S&P 500 is an unmanaged index that is generally considered representative of the U.S. stock market. The performance of an unmanaged index is not indicative of the performance of any particular investment. All S&P returns sourced at StandardandPoors.com.

> The floor in an IUL is a protective and conservative feature. It's ensures that you never interrupt compounding.

When the market crashed in 2008, you would not have lost money in the Index Universal Life contract. When the market dipped in 2015, same thing. Your account would not have gained anything, but it would not have lost anything either. That's the safety net.

The Cap

The interest earned in the Index Universal Life policy is based on the performance of the stock market with a limitation called, the "cap." It's the highest percentage of interest that can be credited to an IUL in any given year.

If the cap is set to 12 percent and the market returns 12.78 percent, the 2010 S&P value, the cash value in the policy would earn the cap, 12 percent.

If the market only returned 11.39 percent, as it did in 2014, or even 3.53 percent, as it did in 2007, then that's the amount the cash value would be credited.

The chart on the right shows how an IUL performed over the past seventeen years with the cap set at 12 percent (a realistic cap based on current capped percentages) versus the stock market based on the S&P 500. It is hypothetical because the caps can change from year to year and are different in various contracts, but this chart shows you what is possible with a 12 percent cap:[12]

---

12   This comparison is for illustrative purposes only and does not represent any particular product. This is not meant to be accounting, legal, or tax advice; seek competent accounting, tax, and legal counsel for specific needs. The Cap and Floor does not include the cost of insurance, commissions nor any other fees. The S&P 500 is an unmanaged index that is generally considered representative of the U.S. stock market and does not include any fees or negative effects of taxation. The performance of an unmanaged index is not indicative of the performance of any particular investment, and no money is invested in the S&P 500. Total Returns Source: Source S&P data: www.standardand poors.com.

Comparison Between S&P Price and
IUL with a Floor (0) and Cap (12)

Starting Account Value $100,000				
Year	S%P Return%	Account Value	ROR	IUL Acct Value
2001	-13.04	$86,960	0.00	$100,000
2002	-23.37	$66,637	0.00	$100,000
2003	26.38	$84,216	12.00	$112,000
2004	8.99	$91,787	8.99	$122,069
2005	3.00	$94,541	3.00	$125,731
2006	13.62	$107,417	12.00	$140,819
2007	3.53	$111,209	3.53	$145,790
2008	-38.49	$68,405	0.00	$145,790
2009	23.45	$84,446	12.00	$163,285
2010	12.78	$95,238	12.00	$182,879
2011	1.00	$96,190	1.00	$184,708
2012	13.41	$109,089	12.00	$206,876
2013	29.60	$141,379	12.00	$231,698
2014	11.39	$157,482	11.39	$258,088
2015	-0.73	$156,332	0.00	$258,088
2016	9.54	$171,246	9.54	$282,710
2017	19.42	$204,502	12.00	$316,635
11 Yr Tot	4.30%	$204,502	7.01%	$316,635

First, notice again how the cap and floor work:

- In 2015, the market dipped below zero, but the account balance did not change. It was credited "0" for that year.
- In 2005, when the market returned 3 percent, the IUL was credited 3 percent.
- When the market did exceptionally well in 2013 with a 29.60 gain, the IUL earned the 12 percent cap.

The cap is determined on an annual basis and is based on how volatile the markets are, and how well the insurance carrier's general account is performing.

Insurance companies' general accounts are managed by some of the most brilliant fund managers in the country. If they earn a conservative interest rate of 4 percent or better on billions of dollars, they have the ability to leverage those returns to be very profitable. This is how insurance companies' guarantee rates of return. It's why we believe that money in an IUL is backed by some of the most powerful and reliable financial institutions in the world.

Over the past seventeen years, the IUL caps have been as high as 17 percent and as low as 8 percent.

Some people ask, "Why would I limit my earnings to a cap of 12 percent when I could earn 28 percent or more if the market goes up?" They are not aware of or don't understand the powerful prevision of the "floor." Look at 2008 when the account didn't lose value and the compounding wasn't interrupted. The account maintained its value instead of losing 38 percent!

> Look at 2008 when the account didn't lose value and the compounding wasn't interrupted. The account maintained its value instead of losing 38 percent!

Without taking into consideration any cost on either side of this comparison—no loads, management fees, taxation, or cost of insurance (figured in an IUL). The numbers work.

And the difference between the final account balances in the chart above illustrate our point.

In the speculative market (another way of saying the stock market), the average interest rate is 4.30 percent. With a cap of 12 and a floor of 0, the average interest rate is 7.01percent.

The difference in value on an account that started with $100,000 is significant.

- The speculative return total is $204,502.
- The cap and floor return total is $316,635
- That's $112,133 *more* using these parameters.
- There's potential to earn more and have more predictable planning for the future. That means more wealth created for future cash flow.

The IUL policy is designed to protect from market losses while providing a competitive rate of return. The concession made for this protection is the IUL participates in the equity index only up to the policy's cap percentage.

Remember, when you lose money in a market dip or crash, it takes longer to recover. If you have a zero floor, you don't have to wait for the market to recover to regain your losses. It's a trade-off that most people gladly make.

The cap and floor in an IUL creates predictability, stability— and a lot less stress. It's a safe, conservative environment. You get to enjoy the upside potential of the stock market with market-linked returns, but you're not going to participate in the uncertainty of the losses.

> The cap and floor in an IUL creates predictability,
> stability—and a lot less stress.

There's one more little perk: each year you gain interest in a stock market account, you are responsible for paying taxes on the gains. **You do not *pay* annual taxes on the gains earned in an IUL.**

No one can predict what the market is going to do. When money is operating between a floor and a cap, however, the climate is somewhat controlled. It provides a tremendous amount of peace, especially when the economy or the stock market tends to be erratic.

> No one can predict what the market is going to do.
> When money is operating between a floor and a cap,
> however, the climate is somewhat controlled. It provides
> a tremendous amount of peace, especially when the
> economy or the stock market tends to be erratic.

Lock and Reset

The cap and floor is your first line of protection against market loss. But insurance companies, being the conservative institutions that they are, have yet another layer of protection in an IUL contract: the "lock-in" of annual gains and "reset" of the annual index value.

It works this way. When interest is credited to the cash value of an IUL account, the cash value and the interest earned combine to become principle, never to be given back, and that value is "locked in." A market dip won't ever deplete the cash value in the policy. This simple illustration and the following scenario communicate the concept.[13]

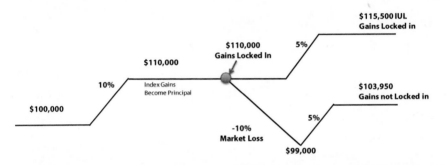

Say you start with a balance of $100,000 and in the first year, the market increases 10 percent. In the IUL, the cash value and the interest combine to become the new principal, never to be given back.

In the second year, the market experiences a 10 percent loss. The IUL maintains the previous year's balance because it is "locked in," but the account exposed to the open market loses $11,000.

---

13   DISCLAIMER: This example is meant to be conceptual. An actual life insurance illustration will show the expenses of the insurance contract, surrender charges, and periods.

The next year, the market does modestly well, 5 percent. The stock-market account goes up 5 percent, but it doesn't make enough to cover the loss.

Because of the lock-in feature, even a small 5 percent increase after a year of being protected from a loss makes a big difference. In this case, it's the difference between having $103,950 versus $115,500. This is why we implore our clients to never interrupt compounding.

How Reset Works

Reset is simply an extension of the lock-in concept. It means the cash value in your policy at the end of the year becomes the new starting value for the next year. This new value is the point from which any gains are calculated for the next twelve months.

This is *very* important! When the stock market takes a loss, it has to recover from its lowest value. But not you. You'll start where the market left off on your policy's anniversary date.

> When the stock market takes a loss, it has to recover from its lowest value. But not you. You'll start where the market left off on your policy's anniversary date.

- If the S&P index value drops 30 percent, your account balance remains at $115,500.
- If the S&P index value shoots to 20 percent the next year, your policy will be credited up to the 12 percent cap.

Think about it. You lost nothing when the market crashed yet reaped the benefit when the market jumped. That's the *power* of the IUL reset!

Think about it. You lost nothing when the market crashed yet reaped the benefit when the market jumped. That's the power of the IUL reset!

Here's what the reset looks like:[14]

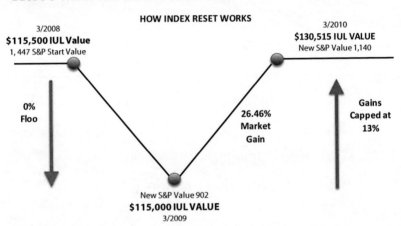

HOW INDEX RESET WORKS

3/2008
$115,500 IUL Value
1,447 S&P Start Value

3/2010
$130,515 IUL VALUE
New S&P Value 1,140

0%
Floo

26.46%
Market
Gain

Gains
Capped at
13%

New S&P Value 902
$115,000 IUL VALUE
3/2009

Because the insurance company resets the index value every year, you have the opportunity to always participate in the upside movement of the market. You can steer clear of market downturns.

Without the reset you're at the mercy of the market roller coaster.

---

14   DISCLAIMER: This example is meant to be conceptual. An actual life insurance illustration will show the expenses of the insurance contract, surrender charges, and periods.

Without the reset you're at the mercy of the market roller coaster. Because the index value is resetting every year, when the market rebounds (and it usually does when there is a major market correction) you get to enjoy earning interest up to the entire policy index cap.

The floor and cap provisions along with the annual lock- in and reset feature in an IUL contract keeps the cash value either making money or protecting the principal. Once the annual interest is credited to the principal, the balance becomes the new principal, never to be subject to loss. This creates the very important true-compounding environment.

> The floor and cap provisions along with the annual lock- in and reset feature in an IUL contract keeps the cash value either making money or protecting the principal.

Mix and Match

There is one more aspect to managing your money inside an IUL. In most IUL contracts, you can mix and match how much money you want to put in a fixed rate of return allocation and how much you want to put in an equity index allocation.

If you think the market is not going to do well in any given year, you can have all your money earning a fixed rate of return. You can put it all back in the indexed allocation when the market rebounds. Or you can do a percentage of each: 25 percent in the fixed and 75 percent in the indexed or a 30 percent/70 percent split. You get to choose. This puts you in the driver's seat with your money. We're sure you'll agree. Control is just as important as safety.

It is important to note that not all IUL contracts are created equal. For example, the cap is different for different companies and different products. Depending on the insurance company, you could have a set cap or no cap at all. We've seen caps set as low as 8 percent, which means that no matter what the market does from year to year, your cap is only 8 percent. We also know of companies that don't set a limit on the cap, meaning the cap is determined by the yearly performance of the stock market index.

> **It is important to note that not all IUL contracts are created equal.**

It follows that the higher the cap, the higher the average your compounding interest will be. Just as there are poorly made cars, middle-grade vehicles, and high-performance machines, IULs can be poorly designed, decent, or high performance.

> **IULs can be poorly designed, decent, or high performance.**

■ ■ ■

Your money can be earning a decent rate of return with uninterrupted compounding. It does not have to suffer any stock-market risk. This ensures cash flow. This is why the Index Universal Life policy is the Wealth Builder account we endorse throughout this book. It is the backbone of Mission ONE Million.

> The Index Universal Life policy is the Wealth Builder account we endorse throughout this book.
> It is the backbone of Mission ONE Million.

Because of these features—the cap and floor, lock-in and reset—we recommend using the IUL as your financial foundation. It offers a secure and predictable footing on which everything else in your financial portfolio can be built.

SEVEN

Cash Flow: How to Use Your Wealth Builder Account Effectively

LET'S REVISIT THE LIST OF PREFERRED BENEFITS FOR OUR money:

1. Earning a decent rate of return
2. No exposure to risk
3. Minimal taxes, if any, on the gains
4. Liquid, or accessible at any time
5. Control of access and distribution
6. No limits on contributions
7. Contributions are tax-deductible

- Number one and two are sustained by the cap and floor/lock-in and reset feature of the Indexed Universal Life policy. With the indexing feature, you can earn a good rate of return. Because your gains are locked in at the end of the year, you are always creating wealth. This assures the most possible cash flow when you decide to retire and start taking distributions. The floor feature offers a safety net, so you're not risking your money.

- Number three is no issue because the IUL is a life insurance policy. All the accumulated gains and distributions are tax favored, meaning there is tax-deferred growth and tax-free distribution.

- Number four and five are convenient features of the IUL. Unlike a qualified plan—401(k), 403(b), or IRA—you are not restricted to accessing the funds because of your age, nor is there a condition to take required distributions at a certain age.

- Number six maximizes your potential. Unlike a ROTH or some other investment vehicles, for most American families, you are not limited on how much money you can place in the IUL annually.

- Number seven is the pitfall, it seems. This feature leads many to fund qualified plans because they believe tax deductible equates to meaning tax free. But let's look at this another way. The premium, or dollars, being placed in the IUL are after-tax dollars. While there is no provision in the tax code to deduct the contributions, we believe it is potentially safer to pay the current income tax. Who knows what it will be in the future?

In all aspects, money is only as good as it facilitates. Whether you're spending, saving, or enduring, the IUL policy facilitates your money's potential very well.

In all aspects, money is only as good as it facilitates. Whether you're spending, saving, or enduring, the IUL policy facilitates your money's potential very well.

The Advantages of Accumulated Cash

Most people have heard the phrase, "Cash is King," but very few understand what it means or how to use accumulated cash to their advantage. You can collateralize accumulated cash, which means you use that cash to secure a loan.

We will share this powerful concept of collateralizing the value of an Index Universal Life policy, and how to use it to optimize cash flow and increase wealth.

If you follow our recommendations, eventually you'll accumulate a reserve of cash in an IUL. This accumulated cash is extremely powerful!

Eventually you'll accumulate a reserve of cash in an IUL. This accumulated cash is extremely powerful!

The IUL contracts we're using have a unique provision called a participating loan feature, which allows the owner to borrow funds from the insurance company for up to 90 percent of the policy's cash value.

You do not borrow the funds from your policy's cash value nor do you interrupt the compounding growth of your policy.

The insurance company loans these funds directly from their general account. They place a lean against your policy's cash value for the dollar amount borrowed and charge a flat interest rate, typically 5 percent.

If the borrowed funds are not paid back before the owner dies, the insurance company will simply cover the loan with a portion of the death benefit and pay the balance of the death benefit to the beneficiary.

Why is this important? Because you have the ability to collateralize the accumulated cash in the IUL to invest in a profitable asset and earn interest on both the new asset purchased and from the index gains in the IUL. All this for a fixed cost of 5 percent. Here is an example:

Let's assume a house becomes available in your local area. For whatever reason, the price is drastically reduced because of foreclosure, tax liens, divorce, or death of the owner. It's worth $180,000 but can be purchased by the first person that shows up with $100,000 cash.

Remember, "Cash is King." You just so happen to have the $100,000 in your Wealth Builder IUL. You notify the insurance company you want to borrow the $100,000 at the 5 percent rate and ask them to please send you the funds. It's that easy to get the money!

Let's also say the house you just purchased with your participating loan can be rented out for $1,000 per month.

After you pay property taxes and insurance, you clear $10,000 per year—a 10 percent return on your $100,000 investment.

> You notify the insurance company you want to borrow the $100,000 at the 5 percent rate and ask them to please send you the funds. It's that easy to get the money!

You just used arbitrage. You paid 5 percent to borrow the funds and earned 10 percent on the newly purchased investment property. That, in itself, is a smart financial move.

But with the IUL's collateral advantage, you have the potential to earn an additional return on the borrowed funds. If you chose to allocate the $100,000 inside the IUL in an index, and earned a 7 percent gain during the same year, the $100,000 in your policy (the same money you used to collateralize the loan) is still earning 7 percent.

In other words, you have two opportunities to grow wealth: a 10 percent gain from the real estate and a 7 percent gain from the index in the IUL. Your only cost would be the 5 percent interest paid to the insurance company for using their money.

The following chart illustrates this scenario.

The ten-year difference is, literally and figuratively, the bottom line: $51,493.

Having funds available when opportunity calls is powerful.

Assumptions

Assumed Asset Return (Rental Income):	10.00%
Assumed Tax Bracket:	20.00%
Amount Invested:	$100,000
Wealth Builder IUL Loan Rate:	5.00%
Wealth Builder Growth Rate:	7.00%

One Year Time Frame		Purchase Using Cash	Using Wealth Builder IUL
Investment:		$100,000	$100,000
	X	10.00%	10.00%
Earnings:	=	$10,000	$10,000
Loan Interest:	-		($5,000)
Taxable Earnings:	=	$10,000	$5,000
	X	20.00%	20.00%
Taxes:	=	($2,000)	($1,000)
Net Investment Earnings:		$8,000	$4,000
Cash Value Growth:	+		$7,000
Net Total Earnings:		$8,000	$11,000
Tax Equivalent Return on Investment:		10.00%	13.75%
Net Internal Rate of Return:		8.00%	11.00%
Effective Increase in Net IRR:			37.50%

Ten Year Time Frame			
Investment:		$215,892	$233,560
Wealth Builder Loan:	-		($162,889)
Subtotal:	=		$70,671
Wealth Builder Gains:	+		$196,715
Net Total:		$215,892	$267,386
		10 Year Difference	$51,493

Using Other People's Money (in this case, the insurance company's general fund), while your money is growing in a protected index account and being leveraged to create wealth, opens the door to becoming financially independent.

One last thing on this concept. You can also use collateralization to your advantage with the bank's money. The IUL insurance contract guarantees you can borrow funds from the insurance company for 5 percent, or whatever their participating loan rate is for that company.

Local banks appreciate the stability of the cash value in your policy and will offer you a line of credit against the cash value in your IUL policy.

> **Local banks appreciate the stability of the cash value in your policy and will offer you a line of credit against the cash value in your IUL policy.**

We always try to negotiate the lowest possible rate. Currently, the lowest rate on a line of credit that's collateralizing liquid cash in an Index Universal Life insurance contract is 3 percent.

If you chose this option (borrow money from the bank) on the $100,000 house, you would be paying the bank 3 percent or $3,000 per year and earning $10,000 net from the rental property.

Remember, the $100,000 would be continually earning gains in the IUL, based on what the Index allocation performance from one year to the next.

The following chart illustrates what all this looks like. It shows the $3,000 paid in interest to the bank and the $10,000 earned from the net rental income. The difference is a $7,000 positive cash flow. We assumed that the $7,000 is not earning any interest. But we did add it to the IUL account value to represent how much this concept increases wealth accumulation. It is hypothetical but having $526,968 at the end of twenty years by leveraging $100,000 is proof that using money wisely can actually pay off!

	Interest Paid to	Net Rental	IUL Average	IUL	Total Wealth
Year	Bank @ 3%	Income	7% Return	Account Value	Accumulation
1	($3,000)	$10,000	$7,000	$107,000	$114,000
2	($3,000)	$10,000	$7,490	$114,490	$128,490
3	($3,000)	$10,000	$8,014	$122,504	$143,504
4	($3,000)	$10,000	$8,575	$131,080	$159,080
5	($3,000)	$10,000	$9,176	$140,255	$175,255
6	($3,000)	$10,000	$9,818	$150,073	$192,073
7	($3,000)	$10,000	$10,505	$160,578	$209,578
8	($3,000)	$10,000	$11,240	$171,819	$227,819
9	($3,000)	$10,000	$12,027	$183,846	$246,846
10	($3,000)	$10,000	$12,869	$196,715	$266,715
11	($3,000)	$10,000	$13,770	$210,485	$287,485
12	($3,000)	$10,000	$14,734	$225,219	$309,219
13	($3,000)	$10,000	$15,765	$240,985	$331,985
14	($3,000)	$10,000	$16,869	$257,853	$355,853
15	($3,000)	$10,000	$18,050	$275,903	$380,903
16	($3,000)	$10,000	$19,313	$295,216	$407,216
17	($3,000)	$10,000	$20,665	$315,882	$434,882
18	($3,000)	$10,000	$22,112	$337,993	$463,993
19	($3,000)	$10,000	$23,660	$361,653	$494,653
20	($3,000)	$10,000	$25,316	$386,968	$526,968

$100,000 Real Estate investment using the Wealth Builder IUL

> ## Having $526,968 at the end of twenty years by leveraging $100,000 is proof that using money wisely can actually pay off!

Income-Tax Free

We know. We spent two whole chapters on how to get out of debt, and now we're telling you it's okay to get into more debt by taking out a policy loan.

A collateralized loan in an IUL is good debt. You're taking advantage of positive arbitrage. But there is yet also another advantage to an IUL policy loan.

We often refer to the IUL as being "tax-advantaged." Here's why:

1. The interest you're earning in your IUL is growing tax-deferred. You aren't getting a 1099 every year on the gains you make.

2. If you take a policy loan, the money is income-tax free.

No one likes to pay taxes. When you take out a collateralized loan on your IUL, the IRS allows you to do it income-tax free. It's a loan, not income, so it is not taxed.

> No one likes to pay taxes. When you take out a collateralized loan on your IUL, the IRS allows you to do it income-tax free.
> It's a loan, not income, so it is not taxed.

You have the option of paying back the loan to the insurance company or having them deduct it from your death benefit when you pass away.

There are other ways to access the cash value in your IUL policy. You can withdraw the interest and leave the principal. If you withdraw the interest the cash value has earned, instead of borrowing it, you will pay income taxes (based on your current income tax bracket for that year).

When you withdraw money out of a policy instead of borrowing it, the withdrawn money can never be returned into the policy. This means you have less cash value in the policy earning uninterrupted compounding.

Whatever you choose to do is totally in your control. You can withdraw or borrow money when you need it—or want it. You can pay it back or choose not to.

> Whatever you choose to do is totally in your control. You can withdraw or borrow money when you need it—or want it. You can pay it back or choose not to.

You can take policy loans to pay for weddings, college, cars, long-term care, or hospital visits. You can take policy loans for down payments on houses. You can invest the money if you want. It's your money. If you've been disciplined about saving, eventually you can spend it the way you want.

> If you've been disciplined about saving, eventually you can spend it the way you want.

Remember when we said you need to put your spending on a diet? This is the reward. When you successfully change the way you eat and exercise, you're healthier; you look and feel great. The payoff is worth the effort.

When you save wisely and effectively use the money, you strengthen your financial health.

When you save wisely and effectively use the money, you strengthen your financial health. You feel terrific—and probably look better too because you're not so worried about your money.

The Advantage of the Death Benefit

Years ago, we met a woman who had inherited quite a bit of money: $2 million. She had plenty of her own money so she wanted her inheritance passed down to her grandchildren. But she was concerned the cash was slowly being consumed by taxes.

When she received her inheritance, she put half in CDs and half in a mutual fund. It was 2010. She had enjoyed a few years of decent gains from the market as it rebounded after 2008, but she also had large tax bills every year from those gains.

Within two years, she had paid over $25,000 in taxes. We asked why she didn't just take money from the mutual fund to pay the taxes. She said, "It's a pain in the neck to call my broker and arrange for the transaction." "And," she continued, "If the market happens to be down on the day the funds are withdrawn, then I lose even more money!" We agreed, and showed her that she was potentially on the path to "sequence of returns risk."

This woman was very savvy in money matters, but she was at a loss for what to do.

> This woman was very savvy in money matters, but she was at a loss for what to do.

We showed her how the IUL worked. Not only would her money be safe while earning decent rates of return every year, she would have more inheritance for her grandkids than the original $2 million. Her death benefit on that original $2 million would be $2.7 million.

When she found out that the $2.7 million death benefit would be given *income tax-free* to her heirs, she didn't hesitate. She moved this money into an IUL.

Not everyone is going to have a $2 million windfall, but this story illustrates the point about the death benefit. Most of us want to leave something behind for our loved ones. Receiving that money income tax-free is an advantage that no other financial institution can offer.

> Most of us want to leave something behind for our loved ones. Receiving that money income tax-free is an advantage that no other financial institution can offer.

Death and taxes are inevitable—as the old saying goes. If you're working and you die prematurely, that death benefit could mean the difference between your loved ones struggling to make ends meet or securing their future.

The death benefit, as we said in the previous chapter, is what makes the IUL life insurance. It can benefit your loved ones when you pass and be leveraged financially while you live. These contrasting qualities make the IUL—as cash-value life insurance—something everyone should seek and understand.

> It can benefit your loved ones when you pass and be leveraged financially while you live. These contrasting qualities make the IUL—as cash-value life insurance— something everyone should seek and understand.

Cost of Insurance versus Management Fees

You might be saying to yourself, "That's all very intriguing, but what about the cost?" The rumored cost of insurance is high—much higher than any other financial vehicle. There is a cost; you pay for the insurance, the death benefit. And it's not as much as you may have heard over the long term.

> There is a cost; you pay for the insurance, the death benefit.

Permanent life insurance, like the stock market, is a long-term arrangement. You can't put your money in for a few years and expect it to do well. If the stock market dips or crashes, it takes time to recover your money. The cost of insurance is more expensive in the first few years. But since this is about creating long-term wealth, it's the long-term costs that should concern you.

In the chart below, we compared the insurance cost of an IUL to the cost of fees and taxes in a managed mutual fund. There is a considerable difference, and you'll be surprised which one is more expensive.

> We compared the insurance cost of an IUL to the cost of fees and taxes in a managed mutual fund. There is a considerable difference, and you'll be surprised which one is more expensive.

We based our comparison on a forty-five year old standard male, saving $12,000 a year in an IUL versus a managed account until age sixty-five. The manage account has a 1.5 percent fee, a 20 percent tax on the gains, earning an average return of 7 percent.

Comparison between Cost of Insurance and Investment Cost—Accumulative

Comparison Between Cost of Insurance and a Managed Investment Acct.			
Year	IUL Cost	Managed Fund Cost	Difference
1	($2,403.00)	($345.00)	($2,058.00)
2	($2,455.00)	($730.00)	($1,725.00)
3	($2,498.00)	($1,118.00)	($1,380.00)
4	($2,533.00)	($1,520.00)	($1,013.00)
5	($2,576.00)	($1,940.00)	($636.00)
6	($2,633.00)	($2,375.00)	($258.00)
7	($2,706.00)	($2,829.00)	$123.00
8	($2,796.00)	($3,300.00)	$504.00
9	($2,898.00)	($3,791.00)	$893.00
10	($2,549.00)	($4,301.00)	$1,752.00
11	($2,695.00)	($4,394.00)	$1,699.00
12	($2,847.00)	($4,570.00)	$1,723.00
13	($2,197.00)	($4,841.00)	$2,644.00
14	($2,344.00)	($5,034.00)	$2,690.00
15	($2,516.00)	($5,237.00)	$2,721.00
16	($2,725.00)	($5,448.00)	$2,723.00
17	($2,725.00)	($5,666.00)	$2,941.00
18	($2,725.00)	($5,894.00)	$3,169.00
19	($2,725.00)	($6,231.00)	$3,506.00
20	($2,725.00)	($6,377.00)	$3,652.00
Total	($52,271.00)	($75,941.00)	$23,670.00

The first six years shows the IUL costs more than the managed investment fees and taxes. We always remind our clients that the costs are going to be more up front. It's what happens after year six that is important.

While the IUL policy costs stay consistent each year for the twenty years of accumulation, the managed fund gets considerably more expensive as the two accounts increase in value. Over the twenty-year history, the IUL's total cost of ownership is $23,670 less than the managed taxable account.

To optimize the value of accumulated cash for distribution later in life, you must reduce the annual cost to manage the funds—not continually increase the cost. We also believe you must eliminate risk at the time of distribution to be able to create a predictable annual cash flow from the accumulated cash. The IUL does this because of the cap and the floor.

After the twenty years of funding, the IUL policy costs drop drastically; it's not nearly as expensive as the managed account. When you stop working and start enjoying the fruits of your earning years, the annual cost of the IUL is minimal, $698 versus $6,634. The IUL policy is ten times less expensive to own than a managed account when the money is needed the most.

Comparison Between Cost of Insurance and a Managed Investment Acct.			
Year	IUL Cost	Managed Fund Cost	Difference
21	($698.00)	($6,634.00)	$5,936
22	($708.00)	($6,900.00)	$6,192
23	($736.00)	($7,177.00)	$6,441
24	($816.00)	($7,465.00)	$6,649
25	($903.00)	($7,766.00)	$6,863
26	($993.00)	($8,078.00)	$7,085
27	($997.00)	($8,402.00)	$7,405
28	($981.00)	($8,739.00)	$7,758
29	($934.00)	($9,091.00)	$8,157
30	($847.00)	($9,455.00)	$8,608
Total	($8,613.00)	($79,707.00)	71,094.00

You can either pay your broker and the government. Or you could retain these savings in your Wealth Building IUL, earning uninterrupted compounded interest, and continuing to create and enjoy wealth.

Making Your Money Last

There are so many advantages to an IUL life insurance policy. That's why we chose it for our Wealth Builder account.

Over the years, we have done countless comparisons between a qualified-plan and an IUL for our clients. Here's a striking example. We had a doctor visit us. He was making $250,000 a year and max funding his 401(k). He was depositing $50,000 a year into his managed retirement fund and planned to quit working at sixty-five.

This is what we found when we ran his numbers:

- He would have to take $192,000 per year from his qualified plan to handle his tax bill and maintain his standard of living.
- His qualified plan would be exhausted when he turned eighty-five.
- If he had the same amount of money in an IUL, and he took out income-tax free policy loans, he would only have to take $154,000 per year.
- Because his cash value would still be in the policy earning interest, he could take that same amount, $154,000 per year, until he was 120 years old, and he would *never* run out of money.

When he found out that he could have used a policy loan to invest in an oil well with his brother five years earlier, he knew it was time to initiate the Mission ONE Million plan.

It was time to get out of debt, put his money in an IUL, and begin creating wealth. He wouldn't have to worry about money anymore. He could get on with life—and maybe pay his brother a surprise visit.

Conclusion

Now You Have a Choice

WE'VE OFTEN HEARD IT SAID, "MONEY ISN'T EVERY-
thing." We agree. But it's right up there with air. In our
daily lives, having access to money can solve a multitude of
problems. That might sound extreme, but it's the truth. Think
about some of the issues you and your family are dealing with
right now. Wouldn't having the ability to write a check make
a big difference?

We've helped hundreds of people who made a choice to
increase their wealth by $1 million. They're on a mission: stay
out of debt and create wealth. They are not wealthy people,
either. They didn't get a $2 million inheritance or even earn
$250,000 a year. However, they do have a few things in com-
mon. They work hard, save well, and spend wisely.

Most importantly, they all made a choice to take control
of their cash flow. It begins with the concepts we bring to light

115

in this book, and a unique financial product, the Wealth Builder Index Universal Life insurance policy.

> Most importantly, they all made a choice to take control of their cash flow. It begins with the concepts we bring to light in this book, and a unique financial product.

The following success stories prove what's possible through the concepts of Mission ONE Million. We want you to note that sometimes people decide to pay off their mortgages in spite of some of the advantages not to. The couple we're about to discuss did so for specific reasons. They chose not to participate in creating arbitrage because they believed they had already created adequate income for themselves.

What you do with your money is important, and all three of these couples have found success using the concepts of Mission ONE Million.

> What you do with your money is important.

Bob and Laura

Bob and Laura were in their mid-sixties. They had quite a bit of savings. Bob was sixty-four but still chose to work. They had paid off half the mortgage on their million-dollar house. The couple was hoping to retire in four to five years, but they knew a $500,000 mortgage would require big payments into their seventies or even early eighties.

It was reasonable to have a six-figure income and a big mortgage, but the two realized that kind of mortgage wouldn't be practical in retirement.

Bob and Laura studied the debt-elimination program. They didn't fully understand it, but they chose to trust the Mission ONE Million concepts.

The Mission ONE Million software program estimated they would be debt-free in four to five years.

The couple came in for their second annual review and proudly informed us that they could pay off their mortgage in two more years! However, they wisely chose to direct that extra cash flow into a Wealth Builder IUL instead.

They had tried other "get out of debt" programs for years, but the Mission ONE Million cash flow management software showed them that even though they were making good income and managing some of their money properly, there were weaknesses in their spending that they hadn't noticed.

> The software not only kept them on track
> with the dates their debts would be paid off
> (which really motived them), but it helped them
> see how they could spend more wisely.

They explained the software not only kept them on track with the dates their debts would be paid off (which really motived them), but it helped them see how they could spend more wisely.

We asked if they felt like they had sacrificed any of their lifestyle to achieve such gain. They said no, and in fact, they bought a lot by a lake and were planning on building a vacation home. They had become more cash-flow efficient and were headed into their retirement years in far better shape than when they started—and it only took a few years!

Jack and Diane

Jack and Diane were in their mid-fifties when they first came to see us. They were retired military living here in Virginia. Prior to that they lived in Jacksonville, Florida, where they still owned a home. The couple had money saved in IRAs and other vehicles. After attending a seminar, they came in and decided to roll some of the IRAs into IULs.

In addition, they had some old Whole Life policies with about $120,000 in cash value they replaced with IUL's.

They were curious about our debt-elimination program because they liked the idea of paying off debt rapidly.

They hoped to retire in ten years, move back to Florida, and pay off the mortgage on that house. They also had a house in Virginia. It had a thirty-year mortgage that they planned to pay off in ten years, leaving them with $100,000 to $150,000 cash. Once they applied that cash against the mortgage on the Florida house, they'd be debt free and could live happily ever after.

They had some credit card debt and a $30,000 car loan, nothing out of the ordinary. They had learned in the seminar that even if their car loan was 0 percent interest, the $500 monthly payment would be better served earning interest.

With the debt-elimination program, they paid off their credit-card debt, then quickly tackled the remaining auto loan. It didn't take long to get those paid off. Then the software focused on the house in Florida, showing it would be paid off in three years instead of twenty-plus.

The house in Virginia Beach which had twenty years left on the mortgage was scheduled to be paid off in only five!

When the couple came back in for an annual review, we asked them if the cash-flow management software had changed their plans (retire in ten years, sell the Virginia house and use the cash to pay off the Florida house). Jack said it had. He and Diane were now considering keeping the property in Florida and using it as a rental because it was going to be paid off so quickly. He could use that money as an income stream.

He was also considering keeping the house in Virginia Beach and renting it out when he and Diane moved back to Florida. It's in a military town, and he believed he could rent it out consistently. Since it would be paid off in five years, he could have another income stream from that.

Jack and Diane expected they would use the debt-elimination software specifically to help them figure out how to pay for—and move to—their house in Florida.

They went from wanting to sell one house after paying off two…to paying off three houses and using two for income!

Now back to the life insurance. IRS Code 1035 allows you to roll old money from a life insurance policy into a new policy. Jack and Diane decided to roll their old Whole Life policy, earning 4 percent interest a year, into an IUL policy that would potentially average 7 percent. In addition to that, the couple planned on putting $19,000 a year into the IUL for growth.

If they continue to do that until they retire, they will earn around $50,000 a year in interest on their cash value. They can take this in policy loans income-tax free.

Jack and Diane can go into retirement debt free and distribute $40,000 to $50,000 or more in tax-free income. They have the two houses paid-off that they will rent, giving them more retirement income. They will continue to enjoy the mortgage deduction on their income taxes because they will be paying the mortgage on their new home.

That tax-free income will allow them to keep more of their Social Security benefits, more of their Military benefits, and more of their distributions from the 401(k)s and IRAs because the money from the life insurance policy is not required to be reported on their tax-return. The policy loans will not have a negative impact on the other accounts.

They will enjoy financial independence in their retirement. Mission…accomplished!

David and Stephanie

David and Stephanie came in to see us a few years ago. He was in his early-fifties; she was in her forties. They wanted to pay off their debts and were looking to retire in about ten to twelve years. Like many people, the couple had some credit card debt and a car loan. They started managing their debts using the cash-flow management software.

Last year, we got a call. David and Stephanie told us they were going to have their debts paid, including their house, in less time than they originally thought. They were in far better shape for retirement than they thought possible. We were curious how long they had been using the software: it was two years in February.

We were elated at their success but still wondered why they had called. Was it just the excitement of achieving their goals or was there something else? In fact, they wanted to know what they should do with the two thousand dollars extra they would have each month once they pay off their mortgage. The two were still planning to work about seven years, and they wanted to know where they should put the money.

We said, "Well, that's just like getting a pay raise." How many people get a $2,000 a month pay raise? We showed them the IUL option, and that's where their money is going.

You can get that kind of "pay raise" if you understand that rapidly getting out of debt improves your cash flow.

When you use this increased cash flow to build your IUL, you, too, can have nicer holidays or better vacations while at the same time put money away for the future. We think that's the epitome of life.

■ ■ ■

There are many people who have made the choice to use our cash-flow management software, get out of debt, and create wealth.

When you're not worried about money, you have the time (and the resources) to make a difference; to realize your potential and, more importantly, your purpose.

We know a single mom who is using the Mission ONE Million strategy to become financially independent. She wants to send her daughter to college. But she also wants to continue volunteering in her community, teaching students their human rights and running an after-school program for inner-city kids who struggle. She doesn't want to worry about money…or losses…or gains…or even the future.

She knows now that she doesn't have to. She made the choice to control her spending, get out of debt, and create wealth. She's obviously spending her time (and her money) wisely. In so many ways, she's living the life that fulfills her.

It comes down to a choice. You can keep living the life of bondage to your lenders, choking or even drowning in too much spending, constantly worried about how you're going to pay your debt, the utility bill, put gas in the car, and buy groceries.

Life as you live it, to a certain extent, has everything to do with the choices you make. You make them one at a time, and they usually come down to making a choice to keep things the same—or to make things better.

Many others have successfully navigated themselves through the Mission ONE Million program, and we know you can too.

Make it your mission. Be ONE of the millions who get themselves out of debt and create wealth.

Imagine what your life will be like when your mission is accomplished. Independence is worth the effort!

And if you remember nothing else, remember this

Your cash flow is most likely the largest asset you will own in your lifetime. It begins to flow when you get your first job or purchase your first investment. How you manage that cash flow will make the difference between coming to the end of your working years with a reserve of cash that can sustain your lifestyle—or trying to figure out how to earn a living until you die.

The four concepts we share in this book are simple yet very powerful ways to optimize your cash flow.

- Manage and minimize your debt with the cash-flow management software.
- Leverage your mortgage to create wealth.
- Use qualified plans wisely.
- Protect your after-tax savings from market risk, experience a competitive rate of return, and eliminate future taxation with the Wealth Builder IUL. It's by far your best choice. And, in our opinion, it is the financial savior of America.

Why I Love Annuities

Steve Burton

For years, specifically through the 80s and 90s, I hated annuities. I had heard such bad things about them like getting poor rates of growth or giving up total control of your money, just to name a couple.

In 2006, a business associate who is a good friend of mine asked me why I didn't sell any annuities. I explained why I didn't like them. The man asked me if I would sit down and talk with him about it. I respected this man because he was knowledgeable about a host of things in the financial marketplace, so I agreed.

In thirty minutes, our conversation had flipped my switch on annuities. Now, they have become a cornerstone of how I help people manage their money more effectively.

In a generation where fewer and fewer have pension plans, people need guaranteed, lifetime income.

The people who are most comfortable in retirement are not necessarily the ones with the biggest bank accounts. Rather, they are those who have more than enough guaranteed income. They have income streams that are more than sufficient to help them live out their lives, in the lifestyle and manner they want. They don't worry about stock market crashes or even the financial impact of the loss of a spouse because they have those guaranteed paychecks in retirement.

Think about this example. Which would you rather have: hundreds of thousands of dollars in the bank or $75,000 coming to you every year, no matter how long that is? Even if you live to be one-hundred years old, you and your spouse will get that income. If you both die, whatever dollar amount that is left in that particular account that is producing this income will pass to your children or grandchildren, or whomever your beneficiaries might be.

Most people would say they would take the income stream.

Why? It's about your retirement income, not just your savings. It doesn't matter how large your savings account is because I've seen people squander their money. I've seen an event like the market crash in '08 take big chunks of their savings away, leaving them at risk to out-live their money in retirement.

The income stream that annuities can provide in retirement is the thing that gives you consistency with your money. If you get nothing else out of this chapter, remember this: retirement is about net income, the money in your pocket month after month. The guaranteed income your annuities provide will always be there, year in and year out. It's money you can fall back on.

Another benefit to annuities is that your money in the annuity is growing tax-deferred. As long as you leave the gains in the annuity, you don't have to pay taxes on the interest until you start taking the money out. Annuities work like qualified plans in that way.

Annuities work well for retirement. The IRS and the government know this, so you can have an IRA or a ROTH IRA annuity. On an IRA annuity, you pay taxes on every penny when you take money out. On the ROTH IRA annuity, you will pay no taxes. Zero taxes. This is my favorite—tax-free.

You can also simply put cash into an annuity, but it's cash that you've already paid taxes on (not tax-deferred as in a qualified plan). However, unlike the ROTH IRA, you will pay taxes on the gains when funding an annuity with non-qualified money.

With all that said, I STILL hate *most* annuities.

I love some, but I hate most. I love annuities that will give a guaranteed income. I hate annuities that put your money at risk.

There are three different types of annuities.

A fixed annuity is like a CD at a bank, but it's with an insurance company. Where a bank in 2018 might be paying 1 percent or less on a five-year CD, you can earn 2 to 3 percent, or even more, in the annuity. A fixed annuity is a fixed rate of interest for a fixed period of time. You aren't going to get rich on that 2, 3, or 4 percent. You probably should not put all of your money in something like this. I have found that if you have too much money sitting in cash or in CDs or money markets, it may be wise to put some of that into a fixed annuity.

Another type of annuity is a variable annuity. Variable annuities have been around for decades. High net-worth people in the 70s and 80s loved these because there were mutual funds inside them. You had the growth of the stock market and the benefits of deferring taxes when the highest marginal tax rates were at 70 percent. People were hoping they would eventually be in a lower tax bracket when they took the annuity income, which made this annuity a tax planning vehicle.

One problem with variable annuities is that they have high fees. The average fee in a variable annuity is over 3 percent, 3.18 percent to be exact. The annuities I like the best have ZERO fees. Also, as we found out in 2001, 2002, and then again in 2008, sometimes those variable annuities can lose a lot of money because they are tied to the ups *and downs* of the stock market.

Indexed annuities, like Indexed Universal Life, are linked to an index like the S&P 500, the Dow Jones Industrial, or others. You have a cap and floor, just like an IUL, so the worst you can do is have a zero rate of return. You can't lose money. If the market goes up 20 percent, you may only get 10 or 12 percent, or whatever cap amount that's set in the annuity contract.

Generally, I like fixed annuities for short-term money and indexed annuities for long-term money.

Indexed annuities give you the protection your money needs from stock market risk, and they provide that lifetime income stream.

Sometimes an annuity may have something called a "rider" attached to them. A rider is an extra service or product feature that you can add on, sometimes for an added fee or cost.

If you want a steady stream of income for the rest of your life, you need an income rider. With this rider, you know exactly what your income will be every year, no matter how long you live. It's that predictable.

This feature in the new generation of annuities is possible with an Income Rider. The benefit will allow a person or married couple to receive "income for life," meaning the income will keep coming no matter how many decades the person lives. Upon death, any remaining money goes to beneficiaries of the policy.

For most annuities with an income rider, once you turn the income on, the income never inflates; it stays the same. So you have to think about that. Things tend to cost more as time goes on, and you need to plan for that. If you live another ten, twenty, or thirty years, is the cost of phone bills, light bills, or groceries going to go up?

The annuities I like best have some inflation protection, meaning the income has the potential to go up as inflation raises prices. But the income stream never goes backwards. Level income is fine, but increasing income, in my opinion, is better.

Some annuities have added riders for long-term care. With the Baby-Boomer generation getting older, many of them are seeing their parents or even themselves needing to go into a nursing-care facility. If they have forgotten to buy or avoided buying long-term care insurance, this will be a huge financial burden.

Some of these annuities have a rider that gives you additional money for long-term care for a specified period of time. Let's say you were getting $40,000 dollars a year in income from the annuity. You have the long-term care rider which doubles your payment for a period of time. Your payment goes from $40,000 to $80,000 for two, three, or five years, depending on the annuity company and that particular rider.

So you get income, you get protection where you can't lose money, and sometimes some pretty decent rates of return. Sometimes with double-digit growth. Paychecks for life. Money goes on to your heirs if you are not around anymore, and you also have the option of the nursing-care riders.

You buy the annuity to cover an income gap. Let's say there's a couple, Bob and Mary, who were going to retire in four or five years. Their Social Security benefits were going to be $40,000 a year, and Bob also has a small pension from his time in the military. Let's say that pension is another $20,000 a year. That gives them $60,000. But they desire to have $80,000 a year in retirement. There is an income gap of $20,000 a year.

I often ask people: do they want that minimum income they need to live comfortably to be hypothetical? Do you want it to potentially run out, to go away and not be there for you to use anymore?

Or would you like to have it go into your bank account, guaranteed every month for the rest of your life?

Here's another point to consider about annuities. Roger Ibbotson is professor emeritus of the practice of finance at Yale School of Management and the respected founder of Ibbotson Associates, a financial research and information firm that was acquired by Morningstar. This guy knows financial research, and he recently published a white paper, "Fixed Indexed Annuities: Consider the Alternative." You know what indexing is from the Index Universal Life. A Fixed Indexed Annuity accumulates interest annually based on a stock-market index. Ibbotson did a historical comparison between Fixed Indexed Annuities and the bond market.

Bonds are a considered a safe alternative to the stock market. What Ibbotson found in his hypothetical return simulation was that the Fixed Indexed Annuity outperformed long-term bonds. The difference was not much—about half a percentage point of interest. But the point he made, which is important here, is that a Fixed Interest Annuity may by an attractive option for retirement savings due to its ability to help cover longevity risk, protect against downside market risk, and still maintain the ability to outperform long-term bonds over time. [15]

WARNING: I HATE the word "annuitization," by the way." One of the reasons I never sold annuities prior to 2006 is that I believed you had to annuitize the annuity if you wanted lifetime income. When you "annuitize," you give the control of the annuity back to the insurance company. They guarantee the income for your lifetime. If you live a long time, it may be a good thing. But if you don't, then the money in the annuity reverts back to the insurance company. That all changed with the invention of the Income Rider, allowing you to receive lifetime income *and not* give up lifetime control of your money to the insurance company.

Mission ONE Million is about ensuring you have an income stream for the rest of your life. Annuities are an important part of the retirement equation because they are the only product available that has the potential for a guaranteed income, and that can cover an income gap nicely.

---

15   Zebra Capital Management. Renowned Economist Roger Ibbotson Unveils New Research Indicating Fixed Indexed Annuities May Outperform Bonds. https://www.prnewswire.com/news-releases/renowned-economist-roger-ibbotson-unveils-new-research-indicating-fixed-indexed-annuities-may-outperform-bonds-over-the-next-decade-300609670.html. March 07, 2018.

So instead of simply dismissing them because you're heard "this" or "that" about an annuity. Find out for yourself how a specific annuity can help you and your family. When you do, I bet that you, too, will say "I love annuities!"

College Without Student Loans

Contributed by Dave Smith

ONE OF THE KEYS TO BEING SUCCESSFUL IS HAVING THE right education. A crucial part of that education is a college degree that centers on your interests, goals, and passions. How can you make that happen in a time when:

- Average Cost of Attendance (COA) is $40,000+
- Average Time to Graduation (Undergrad) is 5.8 years
- Average Cost of a Degree (Undergrad) is $232,000
- Average Student Loan Debt in U.S. is $30,000+

The S-A-F-E Way

We have developed a process that helps parents and their children, working in concert to obtain the best, most relevant education possible with the minimum out-of-pocket expense as possible. By following our guide to Selection, Acceptance, Funding, and Execution, you will be well on your way to obtaining the relevant education necessary to be successful in today's world.

Selection

The first critical step is to align your student's unique talents and abilities with an elite, selective, or competitive school that will offer attractive admissions and financial aid packages.

There are approximately 2,000 non-profit institutions in the U.S. College and university system. There is a specific breakdown of how schools are ranked. Schools such as Stanford, Harvard, MIT, Duke, Vanderbilt, Yale, and Pomona are some of the 50 "Elite" schools. Next are "Selective" schools made up of roughly 150 institutions including USC, Cal, UCLA, Santa Clara, Cal Tech, and Pitzer. The third category is made up of approximately 250 "Competitive" colleges such as Pepperdine, USD, Occidental, LMU, and UC Davis. The remaining 1,750 are basic, standard colleges such as state schools and universities.

The sheer number of students following the herd mentality of attending state and local colleges reduces the amount of merit based and academic awards available there. Elite, selective, and competitive colleges typically perceived as too expensive or exclusive have ample means of discounting their tuition for those students deemed as desirable. Merit-based aid has no income requirement or limitations; it's the school's subjective decision. The more valuable your student is to them, the more they will discount their services in order to secure their attendance.

Selecting the right college requires a thorough analysis of multiple factors that are unique to your student's career objectives and lifestyle. Using their time in high school to develop interests and to make connections to a possible career path is one of the most effective ways for your student to fine-tune their decision-making process. Rather than arbitrarily deciding to be a doctor or a lawyer, this process helps them gain a better perspective of what they are truly interested in. It allows them to gain an understanding of what their career path entails and the options that are available within it.

No other decision has such lasting academic and financial impact as the choice of the college your student attends. Most families use emotional criteria such as a school's proximity to home, school reputation, or even the best football team to pick a school and just assume that the student will fit in. They are not aware that there are schools out there that will be a good fit based on class size, major offerings, environment, and overall attitude.

Here's a quick review of what needs to happen before your student begins to fill out an application form:

- Set the expectation—In families where college is an expectation from an early age, students rise to the challenge and select colleges, majors, and careers, and usually finish college in four years.
- Fit, Fit, Fit—An education that fits your student's goals, aspirations, talents, and personality is priceless. This leads to happiness, contentment, higher productivity, and eventually to just the right career. Keep your eyes open for the clues.

- "Why" is more important than "How"—Your student needs to answer; Why am I going to college; why should I put out the effort; why is it important? This helps provide the motivation necessary for a successful college experience.
- Utilize all of the available tools—Science-based selection programs, volunteer activities, and job shadowing. Thorough preparation helps guarantee success.

Acceptance

Although the institution makes the final decision regarding acceptance or rejection of the admission applications, knowing and then utilizing some of the selection criteria can put your student at the top of the list.

Let's change the paradigm. It's vital to replace the common mindset of "How can my student compete?" with "Which colleges are willing to compete for my student?"

While a central part of the admission process is to know which colleges your student prefers, you can take it a step further and apply to colleges of equal quality that compete for the same students. Research can uncover these "unknown" colleges that will provide award letters that your student can use as leverage. Test scores and GPAs are just starting points or the common denominator among applicants. Tagging, legacies, and demonstrable interest play an important role in the acceptance process.

Tagging

A "Tag" is a positive mark added to a student's admissions application that indicates that he or she is of special interest to the college. Children of alumni get tags known as "legacies," the size of the tag or size of their advantage is usually measured by the depth of the parent's generosity to the school. Students with special talents also get tagged. Students with outstanding academic qualities, athletic abilities, or musically/artistically-inclined students are of special interest to the colleges.

Your student's intended school may need three tuba players for the marching band and have a glut of saxophone players. This may not help your saxophone-playing student, but be aware that sometimes it's enough of an advantage to help them get in at competing, equally attractive institutions. Having more than one school choice gives your student an edge because the other school just may need another saxophone player.

Underrepresented minorities, sexes, and students from underrepresented states receive tags. Based on federal funding requirements, your student may receive a tag if they are female, male, from a certain state, etc.

Once an application is tagged, the individual is removed from the common pool of applicants and moved to an entirely new level for special consideration. An applicant that normally may not have been looked at twice may find that being tagged opens many doors. It's vitally important to know in advance which colleges give extra attention to specific tags.

Packaging

Imagine looking out over a cornfield. There are thousands of stalks of corn all planted in neat, evenly-spaced rows. Now imagine that several of these stalks are three feet taller than the rest. Help your student stand out like those taller stalks amid all of the remaining freshman applicants and you make it easier for the admissions officer to find them.

College is big business loaded with rules and procedures geared to help fill their classrooms with students that have a high probability of success. The key to making your student one of the desirable ones is by promoting their value to each school. Make it obvious to the school that your child is the one that they have been looking for.

You must "Package & Position" your student based on the College Acceptance Profile (CAP) that is unique to each school. The students with the highest CAP scores are most attractive to colleges and are eligible for the best financial aid packages. These students receive more grants and free money versus them having to obtain student loans and participate in work-study programs.

The CAP criteria used by selective and elite institutions include:

- Awards—National, Regional, State, County, and School

- Academics—Standard Test Scores
- Activities—School and Outside (Leadership is important)
- Community Service—Volunteerism, Helping Others
- Character Traits—Teacher/Counselor Ratings

Admissions committees rely on CAP to objectively review each applicant and then compare them to the established selection criteria for the school. In a survey by the National Association of College Admission Counselors, 54 percent of the colleges that responded said that they use preferential packaging.

Funding

Financial aid can be made up of these sources:

- Need-Based
- Merit-Based
- Scholarships
- Endowments

College costs money...whether it's your money, the government's money, or the school's money depends on smart strategy and a winning formula. Since the goal is for your student to attend a great school without student loans, the first step is to understand Need-based Financial Aid. Applying for need-based aid is essential even if you don't think that you're eligible because many schools won't even consider your student for "non-need" based aid if you don't apply. This is done through the Free Application for Federal Student Aid (FAFSA) which is available online at www.fafsa.ed.gov.

The Higher Education Act of 1965 states that it is the parents' responsibility to educate their children beyond the twelfth grade. The law states that if a family can demonstrate "need," the government will assist in paying for the education. The good news is "need" is not subjective but is based on a formula, and you can estimate your contribution much easier by understanding the calculation.

The financial aid administrator at each school develops the average Cost of Attendance (COA) for all categories of students. The COA = Tuition & Fees + Room & Books + Transportation + Miscellaneous Expenses. The law also provides limited allowances for computer expenses, dependent care, and expenses for handicapped students. The COA can vary for each student at the same school but students in the same situation must have the same COA.

The next part of the formula is the Expected Family Contribution (EFC), which is the amount you as a family are expected to contribute toward your student's education expenses and is recalculated each academic year during the FAFSA process.

After subtracting your EFC from the college's COA, the remainder is "need." Your EFC is the same at every college but your need at each college will vary according to the college's COA. If your EFC is $10,000 and COA at college A is $13,000 and college B, which happens to be an elite school, is $43,000 it may make perfect sense to choose college B. FAFSA is just the first step of the funding process, however.

Once your student has filed the FAFSA you are able to explore various financial aid opportunities that can make the difference between affording your student's first choice school and having to settle for less. It has been estimated that an excess of $60 billion is available every year that goes untouched by students.

In many cases parents assume that scholarships, monies distributed by entities such as civic organizations or corporations, are the key to making up the difference for them financially. These funds are paid directly to the student to offset the cost of college but they represent less than 3 percent of the total money available for education. A college plan that counts on scholarships to pay the majority of costs is an ill-fated strategy that will have disastrous results for most families.

Merit-based aid is an incentive to attract students considered valuable to the institution in the "subjective" areas of academics, arts, athletics, or outside activities. Merit awards are distributed by the Admissions Office of each school in the form of distributional discounts and loans subsidized by endowment funds. Colleges control over $150 billion in endowment funds, the second- largest pool of money behind Federal Aid, meaning they are choosing who gets this money. Properly positioning and demonstrating the value of your student is imperative if you want to make college affordable today.

Because private schools generally exhibit the highest COA, many families eliminate them, believing that they cannot afford the high expense. While this thinking seems reasonable, it is faulty thinking. Private institutions have the largest endowment funds available and therefore offer the largest awards to students that meet or exceed the school's criteria.

Accessing this additional money at selective and elite schools may require more effort but is certainly worth it. The keys to properly position your student includes them achieving strong scores on the SAT or ACT, maintaining contact with the Department Chairman at their selected schools, and demonstrating their direction and focus along with the other qualities potential schools are searching for.

As you discovered in *Mission ONE Million*, if you plan early enough and have enough cash value built up in your policy, you would be able to finance your student's college tuition through income-tax free policy loans.

Execution

Now that you have an inside look at how desirable schools will compete for your student, it's time to use that information to your student's best advantage. It's time to implement the plan that hopefully has been in place since your student's sophomore year in high school.

Applying early is a form of demonstrable interest and typically results is a favorable review from admissions. It is a great strategy and can be used as leverage against other schools with attractive offers. In essence, the longer your student waits to apply, the fiercer the competition becomes for the remaining seats. With an admissions process that is both objective and subjective in a highly competitive environment, the odds of success increase dramatically as your student ferrets out the ideal fit from the good fits that we discussed in the Selection section.

Working ahead of schedule allows your student time to fine tune the applications and get valuable unhurried input from counselors or professionals. Requesting high school transcripts, letters of recommendation, and SAT/ACT scores all take time to coordinate. Exceeding deadlines can work wonders in getting a school's attention and it also takes the pressure off you and your student.

Timeline:

- **Freshman & Sophomore Year**—Focus on SAT/ACT preparation and fine tune career interests.
- **Junior Year**—Continue preparation for SAT/ACT. Participate in volunteer and extracurricular activities that will strengthen their overall profile.
  - **January through May**—Refine list of schools to apply to and ensure a good fit.
  - **Summer**—Obtain requirements plus all admission applications and begin to complete them and work on the required essays.

- **Senior Year**—Continue participation in volunteer and extracurricular activities.
  - **September**—Fine tune applications and request letters of recommendation from teachers, counselors, coaches, and mentors.
  - **October**—Submit applications and begin applications for financial aid.
  - **November & December**—Contact potential schools and arrange for personal visits and interviews.
  - **January**—Submit the FAFSA & CSS profile.
  - **February & March**—Follow up with potential schools and schedule personal visits with additional schools if desired.
  - **March**—Acceptance/Waiting List/ Denial letters will start arriving.
  - **April**—Student Aid Report (SAR) awards and offers of acceptance from individual schools will begin to arrive. Review each SAR for accuracy and notify the school's department of admission prior to end of month.
  - **May**—Commit to the school of choice.

Through the S—A—F—E process you and your student will exercise due diligence, carefully consider what constitutes a good fit, apply with confidence, and then have the opportunity to choose between attractive offers made by your collection of ideal schools.

Getting the right education is not a four-year decision but a decision that will help guarantee a lifetime of success!

Learn more about College Without Students loans and to let us know how helpful this information has been please visit us and give us your feedback at: www.TheSafeSteps.com.

"Remember the Lord your God, for it is He who gives you the ability to produce wealth."

—Deuteronomy 8:18

About the Authors

Merle Gilley is the founder and president of TriQuest USA and has  been a successful life insurance agent since 2003. He has become one of the nation's leading professional trainers in the financial services industry as a Life insurance expert. Merle has spent the last decade supporting his personal clients as well as training several thousand financial service professionals to understand the value of working with a solid financial model.

Steve Burton is the founder and president of Equity 1, Inc. Financial  Solutions and is partners with Merle Gilley at TriQuest USA, serving as the VP of Marketing and Sales. For over 15 years, Steve has been helping individuals across the country take control of their financial future and provide a financial legacy for their families. He has educated thousands through his radio shows, books, and seminars on how to grow and protect money.

Mission One Million

is for anyone who wants to

get out of debt,

build wealth,

and become financially independent.

You don't have to be wealthy to build wealth.

If you want to find out more information about Mission One Million, visit

www.MissionOneMillion.com